The 5 Secrets of a Phenomenal Business

How to Stop being a Slave to Your Business and Finally Have the Freedom You've Always Wanted

Howard Partridge

Sound Wisdom
P.O. Box 310
Shippensburg, PA 17257-0310

For more information on foreign distribution, call 717-530-2122.
Reach us on the Internet: www.soundwisdom.com.

ISBN 13 TP: 978-1-9378-7943-3
ISBN 13 Ebook: 978-1-9378-7944-0

For Worldwide Distribution, Printed in the U.S.A.
2 3 4 5 6 7 8 / 17 16 15 14

Contents

Dedication

To the late Zig Ziglar.

Zig, you inspired millions. I am grateful and honored to help carry your legacy forward. I'll see you - and yes, I do mean you - not just at the top, but hey, I'll see you OVER the top!

Foreword by Tom Ziglar

"Will You Partner With Us?"

In 2007, our top sales lady Margaret Garrett came into my office and said, "Tom, there is a businessman in our conference room you need to meet." After 45 minutes of sharing our stories and asking each other questions, it became clear to me that this guy was different. Not only was it obvious that he was a big Zig fan, but he had the same mission that we had—to make a difference in the lives of others. That was the beginning of one of the most fulfilling personal and business relationships I have ever had. Today, I claim Howard Partridge as my business partner, my friend, and my brother.

As our relationship grew, Howard invited my dad to speak at one of his conferences for business owners. It was a huge success for both of us and Howard continued to invite us back. From 2007 to 2010 I was able to attend several of Howard's events, and he even asked me to speak! Each time I went I was more impressed. Not just with Howard, but with the business owners in his group, too. In a nutshell, they were *real*. Real people with real families, real problems, real opportunities, and real dreams. Some in the group had been business owners for 40 years, others were brand new. Some were trying to figure out how to turn their "job" back into the "dream" they had when they started their business. Others were working hard on systemizing their business so that they could leave it as a legacy for their kids. And some of the long-time members of Howard's group were helping the others. Why? Because they could! They had gone through the process and now had turn-key businesses, which meant they had the time and resources to do what they wanted to do.

If you know me you know that I am a little reserved. I like to observe and ask a lot of questions. I started asking these business owners what they liked about Howard Partridge. In almost every case I got the same three answers:

1. **I love Howard.**

2. **Our business is making substantially more money than it ever has.**

3. **I have more time to spend with my family.**

As a Ziglar, I have to tell you that Number 3 got me excited. Financial success is very important, but no amount of success is worth sacrificing your family. Howard was teaching business owners how to achieve both personal and professional success. Not only that, but he was using many of our programs in the process!

In January of 2011 it became clear that Dad's health would no longer allow him to travel and speak publicly. At 84, his incredible career was winding down. In February of 2011 my two sisters, my niece and I went to Chicago to spend a 14-hour day with a consultant whose specialty was looking at *all* of the assets of a business and then recommending opportunities that may have been overlooked. We went because we are committed to carrying on Dad's legacy, and we know that we have to do this in new and different ways. At the end of the exhausting meeting, the consultant said we had a huge opportunity in a new market for us—Small Business Owners. He said small business owners already believe what Zig Ziglar teaches, and what they need is a system and a coaching program to help them grow their businesses because success as a small business owner is the combination of being the right kind of person and implementing proven business systems.

We agreed 100 percent, but we had two big problems—we didn't currently do coaching, and we didn't have a complete business system developed.

Before we left Chicago our family started talking about Howard Partridge. Howard had been doing exactly what we had been wanting to do for nearly 15 years. He had a proven track record and we had been working with him for over three years. We had seen it with our own eyes. On the way back from Chicago it was decided that I would call Howard.

The Call: "Will you partner with us?"

I called Howard and gave him the background of our Chicago meeting. Then I popped the question. "Howard, we are going to start working with small business owners—will you partner with us?"

To say that Howard was excited was an understatement. He readily agreed. But I still had one more huge question for him. Our company, our brand, our legacy, our name, depends on one thing—our reputation. "Howard," I asked, "what happens if someone joins our program and it's just not a fit for them? What do you do? How do you handle it?"

Without hesitation he answered, "We make it right." I was glad he got that answer right! Now, over two years later, Howard and I have done over 50 events together all across America. We have spoken together in the United Kingdom and in Australia. Guess what? Those who join us are getting incredible results. And even those who turn out not to be a fit, well, Howard makes it right, just like we make it right.

As you read and devour *The 5 Secrets of a Phenomenal Business*, I encourage you to take notes and then implement into your own business what Howard teaches. Why? Simple, really—it works.

Tom is uniquely qualified to bring the Ziglar philosophy and wisdom to your business. For 48 years Tom has steeped himself in the techniques of living a successful life and running a successful business. He is the CEO of Ziglar, Inc., and the proud son of Zig Ziglar. Prior to being named CEO, Tom began his career in retail and direct sales. He joined the Zig Ziglar Corporation in 1987, learning every aspect of the business as he climbed from working in the warehouse, to sales, to seminar promotion, to sales management and then on to leadership.

Visit www.ziglar.com for more information.

Introduction

Do you remember *why* you went into business for yourself?

Was it to make a lot of money? Or was it to "be your own boss"…to "chart your own course"…to have a little more "free" time?

Yeah, right!

The brutal reality of most small business owners' lives is that you feel like a slave to the business. There's very little family time, major stress, no real freedom, the business consumes your minds 24/7, and you feel like you have a "job" rather than a business. Your days are consumed with putting out "brush fires."

Can you relate to that? I sure can.

My Story—From the Trunk of My Car to Living the "American Dream"

I'm originally from L.A. (Lower Alabama!). I grew up on welfare in Mobile, Alabama, where there were seven kids crammed into a little 600-square-foot shack. The roof on that house was so bad that every time it rained, we had to get out all the pots and pans to catch the leaks.

My mama somehow fed us on $100 a month from the welfare department. I still remember getting Christmas presents from the social workers.

When you grow up like that, how are you likely to turn out? For me, I was an 18-year-old rebellious teenager with hair down to my shoulders. I got in a fight with my stepdad and he kicked me out!

My friend and I scraped up enough money for me to get a Greyhound bus ticket to Houston, Texas. This is where my real dad lived—he left when I was a year old and I had only met him twice in my entire life. My sister was there with him, and I figured I needed a change.

When I stepped off that Greyhound bus, I actually had only 25 cents in my pocket. And that was *all* the money I had to my name! I wasn't even sure my dad would be there for me—but he was, and I lived with him and his wife for about a year.

After a few odd jobs, I became a professional waiter and worked in high-end restaurants where I presented flaming tableside cooking, wearing a tuxedo. I learned how to make a lot of great dishes at the table—Steak Diane, Pepper Steak, Caesar Salad Dressing from scratch, Hot Spinach Salad, Bananas Foster, Cherries Jubilee, and many more. Setting stuff on fire *inside* was very cool indeed!

During my years as a waiter, I learned a great deal about the customer service experience. I've always been an entrepreneur at heart. As a kid, I cut grass, picked up pine cones, sold stuff door to door, and did anything I could to make money.

As a waiter, I made just enough to pay the rent.

Then I met my wife—Denise Concetta Antoinette Pennella. Now, *that's* Italian! I went to New Jersey to marry Denise, and when you marry into an Italian family, you don't get wedding presents like dishes, toasters, and blenders. Instead, what do you get? You get CASH!

We received $3,000 in wedding money! While we were in New Jersey, a friend of the family who was my age (23 at the time), was tooling around in a little red Mercedes convertible. I said to myself, *I want to know what THAT guy does, and I want to know if it's LEGAL!* Turned out he owned a business. So as soon as we returned to Houston, I spent all of our wedding money to start my first business—out of the trunk of my car. My wife was really thrilled about that, let me tell you!

After being in business for 13 years, I felt like a slave to my business. I loved to travel, but when I did, much of the "vacation" was consumed talking to customers and employees back home.

Do you know what I'm talking about? Do you have to take your appointment book and cell phone with you wherever you go?

Two Secrets that Changed My Life Forever

After spending 13 long years becoming a slave to my business, I learned two big secrets that changed my life forever. My mentor would come to my office once a week to talk and pray with me. He noticed how involved I was in every little detail of the business and how dependent it was on me; he recommended I read *The E-Myth Revisited* by Michael E. Gerber.

That book changed my business and my life forever.

After reading *The E-Myth,* I took a week off and traveled to my favorite place in the world, Destin, Florida, and sat on the beach and re-created my future. The first secret I learned was that you've got to have systems set up in your business if you don't want to be a slave to it. I learned how to work *on* the business instead of just *in* it as *The E-Myth* says.

The second secret I learned (also from *The E-Myth*) is that the only reason your business exists is to be a vehicle to help you achieve your LIFE GOALS. You went into business for yourself because you had a dream of having more time for your family—a dream of doing *what* you want *when* you want. Instead, you sometimes feel like a slave to the business.

That's what I felt. I was literally a prisoner of my own making. Don't get me wrong, I really enjoyed serving my customers and doing the technical work of the business, but now I saw a different picture.

I saw that I could have a turnkey business—one that works just as well *without* me as it does *with* me. I returned to Houston and started working on the business from my new perspective, and we grew it into a multimillion dollar turnkey enterprise. I have 40 staff members who love their work, which allows me to do what I love to do—assist small business owners become phenomenally successful.

In 1998, I began teaching my systems to other business owners through information products, seminars, and coaching. As it turns out, I was speaking at the same convention as Michael E. Gerber (author of the book that changed my life, *The E-Myth Revisited)*. The seminar promoter arranged for us to meet over breakfast.

Since that breakfast meeting in Las Vegas, Michael has not only presented at my live events, he has become a great friend and mentor to me. I talk to him several times a year, and I will always be grateful to him for changing my business life. I love Michael; he is a brilliant, incredibly gifted man.

Since that time I have owned eight small businesses, had partners, bought and sold businesses, worked in network marketing, and even started a franchise operation. My live events have included world-famous American legend Zig Ziglar and best-selling authors Tamara Lowe (Get Motivated!, the largest business seminars in the world, with her husband, Peter), Bob Burg (author of *Endless Referrals* and *The Go-Giver*), Dr. Joseph A. Michelli (author of *The Starbucks Experience*), and others. And I have been recognized by Dr. John C. Maxwell, the number one leadership expert in the world.

I am especially grateful for my relationship with the Ziglar Corporation. I have been blessed to not only share the stage with Zig and to be featured on his live video webcasts, but to enjoy a close personal relationship with the entire Ziglar family and team. I recently launched Ziglar's very first coaching program for business owners. Tom Ziglar and I have been traveling the world helping small business owners get free.

✳✳✳

Some years ago, when my business was still very small, I was part of a local industry group that met every week to talk about ways to improve our businesses. There were about a dozen people who met every Monday morning. They complained about the economy and how customers wouldn't pay their price. They had what Zig called "stinkin' thinkin'" and they needed a "check-up from the neck up"!

Some of them were wearing cut-off blue jeans, flip-flops, and hadn't shaved, and they wondered why they didn't have much business. I strolled in carrying a briefcase and wearing a sport coat and tie—and a positive attitude. They actually laughed at me and said, *"Who do you think you are, Zig Ziglar or somebody?"*

The funny thing is I did not know Zig Ziglar at the time. Little did they know they were speaking my future! Today I have the pleasure of not only working with the Ziglar organization, but the thrill of helping small business owners around the world achieve record sales and profits while having more time off.

And that is what I want for you. That is what this book is all about—helping you stop being a slave to your business by transforming it into a predictable, profitable, turnkey operation so you can live out the *one and only reason* your business exists…

Chapter 1

The *One* and *Only* Reason Your Business Exists

The greatest business lesson I ever learned is that my business exists for *one* and *one* reason *only*. And your business exists for the same reason: *to be a vehicle to help you achieve your LIFE goals!*

The everyday demands of a business can have a dramatic impact on your personal lives. The good news—no, *phenomenal* news—is that the impact can be *positive!* It doesn't have to be negative. So, the first step toward a phenomenal business is to understand *why* it exists—to enhance your life. To be a vehicle that takes your life from where it is to where you want to go.

We go into business because we have a dream. We have a dream of working for ourselves and having more free time. But then we get sucked into the constant demands of the business. Before too long, we are enslaved by it.

The key is to *design your life goals first.* In my first published book, *7 Secrets of a Phenomenal LIFE,* I share that LIFE stands for Living In Freedom Every day. You must have a vision for what freedom looks like to you.

One of the tools we use is the Wheel of Life that has the seven core areas of life. You rate yourself on the seven areas on a scale of 1 through 10. You assess your life as it is now and compare each area to what you want it to look like.

Develop a Vision First

If you don't have a clear vision for the life you want, you won't build the right kind of business. You *must* get the fact that your business works for you. You don't work for the business. Your business is a *vehicle* to help you live out your life goals. It's *the vehicle* you have chosen. You design the business to facilitate your life goals.

Don't get me wrong, you will still work just as hard—and if you don't have money, you may have to invest more "sweat equity" than you ever imagined to get it where you need it to be. You may have to work long and hard in the beginning. But if you design your life goals *first* and build your business around that vision, you will avoid being a slave to your business. Your business will add to your life instead of taking away from it.

When I first read *The E-Myth Revisited*, I finally understood how to stop being a slave to my business. Michael Gerber talks about the *primary aim*. When you design a compelling, purposeful, phenomenal picture for your life and design your business around your life goals, you will approach your business with more purpose and direction.

You will have a compelling *reason* to build it. With a compelling vision for your life, you are willing to learn what you need to learn and, more importantly, implement it.

The other side of the proverbial coin is that your personal habits also have a dramatic impact on your business. To grow a phenomenal business, you've got to become a phenomenally successful person with positive habits. Just knowing how to build a business is not enough. I encourage you to read my book, *7 Secrets of a Phenomenal LIFE,* to discover how to have a phenomenal life.

Chapter 2

GPS for Phenomenal Success

Have you ever used a GPS (Global Positioning System)? Of course you have. GPS is used by many to get from "here to there" these days. When I started my business 28 years ago, we used something called a "map," and it was made of this interesting material called paper!

But today, we simply get out our smart phones (that knows where you are…scary), and open our maps application. Or we get out our Garmin and type in where we want to go. It knows where you are, and gives you turn-by-turn directions to get you to your destination.

Do you know where you want to go? Are you clear about where you want to go in life and in business? And more importantly—do you really know *where* you are *now?*

The first thing a GPS does is determine where you are. I had the amazing honor of being quoted in the last chapter of the last book Zig Ziglar wrote, *Born to Win*. And I helped Tom Ziglar put together a phenomenal business assessment that reveals exactly where you are in your business right now. The assessment in *Born to Win* asks ten questions under each of these important five areas of business:

1. *Marketing* - Everything you do to attract prospects to your business.

2. *Sales* - Everything you do to convert prospects into paying customers.

3. *Operations* - Everything you do to serve your clients.

4. *Administration* - Everything you do to track your numbers and the internal office systems to run the business.

5. *Leadership* - Everything you do to lead and guide your business.

The assessment reveals how solid your systems are in each area (or not). You find out where you really are in your business. Most small business owners don't really understand how to assess where they are. The answers to these questions reveal *where you are* in your business compared to where you want to go, and that is extremely important.

In fact, in coaching small business owners for many years, I've found that most don't really have a grasp on where they really are in their business. This assessment helps you see where your business really is right now.

Back to GPS. Let's say I want to go to my favorite spot in Florida, but I have been blindfolded, driven around for hours, and dropped off on the side of an unmarked road. Unless I know where I am, I can't get to Florida. The GPS picks up where I am. Then I can type in the location in Florida and it will give me step-by-step directions to get there.

So, the first part of *GPS for phenomenal success* is allowing the GPS to determine where you are. Once you know where you are, you can then use GPS to guide you to your destination:

GPS—Goals, Plans, Systems

G is for Goals. Without clearly defined goals, you will never know where you are going, or if and when you get there. You must have clearly defined life goals and business goals. They must be written down. They must be yours.

They must be meaningful to you. They must be specific and measurable. And of course, this entire book could be about setting goals, but you get the point.

P is for Plans. You need a map. Would you try to go somewhere you've never been without a map? A simple business plan that includes your *business goals,* your *mission,* a 12-month *budget,* and a *marketing plan.* It sounds like a lot, but I'll show you how to make it really simple. It is vital that you create a really good map and follow it closely.

S is for Systems. You must choose what vehicles you will use on this amazing and exceedingly important journey. Your business is a vehicle; and like any vehicle, it has a number of systems that work together to operate it. A bicycle has the wheel system, the gears, the frame, the braking and steering systems, all working together as a system. An automobile has a number of systems such as the combustion system, the drivetrain system, and the steering system that work together.

A Boeing 747 aircraft has many systems that work together and can take a *bunch* of people a long way! I created a "747 Business Model" that is in Chapter 4 of my book *7 Secrets of a Phenomenal LIFE.*

The five systems of a phenomenally successful business make up the vehicle you will use to get to where you want to go. They are also the systems that will help you stay there. The stronger the systems, the smoother they work together, and the better your trip will be. It's no fun running out of gas or breaking down on the side of the road. It's no fun having to rely on a vehicle that is falling apart, which is the case for many small businesses.

So, set your **G**oals. Develop your **P**lan. And build **S**ystems in your business. The rest of this book will help you do that.

Chapter 3

How to *Stop* Being a *Slave* to Your Business

and Transform It Into a Predictable, Profitable,
Turnkey Operation

If you have staff, you are probably familiar with the story of Somebody, Everybody, and Nobody:

> Somebody was asked to do something that was Everybody's job. Everybody thought Somebody was going to do it, but Nobody did it. When Nobody did it, Everybody asked why Somebody didn't do it. Somebody said it was Everybody's job. Everybody said it was Nobody's job, therefore Nobody did it.

Can you relate to that story? If you don't have staff, this chapter will reveal how not having staff is holding you back and what to do about it.

Why Systems are Critical to Your Business

The key to profitable growth

Have you ever seen companies that grow big fast only to discover that more money is going *out* than is coming in? I have. And it is *not* very phenomenal! The bigger you get without systems, the more money is going out the door in reinventing every day.

Employees perform better

When your employees don't have to depend on you to direct their every move because they have a system to work in, their performance increases.

Fewer surprises

Have you noticed that human beings do weird things? The stuff people come up with sometimes is mind boggling. Like the time one of my clients had an employee who wrecked a company truck. Instead of calling the owner and letting him know, he hid the truck behind his house and didn't show up for work the next day. Of course my client didn't have systems in place then. Now he does. Don't leave it to your employees to try and figure out the best thing to do. Have a system.

Keeps the owner in line

I don't know about you, but I like to change things, update them, and try something new from time to time. As the owner, you may like to tinker, or you decide which part of the system you feel like using that day. As the owner, you have to be the example and follow the procedures yourself if you want your staff to follow them.

Many years ago in my service business, I went out to do an on-site presentation for a prospective client. I assumed that the client wouldn't buy and did not write up a proposal. Instead, I just quoted a verbal price and left. Sometime later, the prospect called to have the work done. My salesperson looked high and low for the paperwork and finally in frustration asked the prospect if she was absolutely sure we had done an on-site consultation.

"Oh yes" she said. "A man drove up in a Lexus, looked around and told me how much it would be!" Of course my sales agent knew exactly who she was talking about—me! The owner—the one who decided not to follow the system that day. And of course there's another lesson there too. Don't judge a prospect. Do the proposal!

If you like to change things around and you have a team, they will be confused if you don't inform them beforehand. Customers may also become confused. When you change something, be sure to communicate it and update the *system*.

A consistent service experience

When you have a system, the customer knows exactly what to expect. McDonald's is the "poster child" for systems because customers can get the same hamburger in Tokyo as they can in Paducah, Kentucky. It may not be the *best* hamburger, but it's the *same* hamburger. It's *consistent* because they have a *system*.

Takes less of the owner's time

The idea behind building systems is so you have more time. If you are "reinventing the wheel" every day because there is no system in place for your team to follow, you end up doing everything yourself. Ultimately, you want to streamline your business so you can have more time to pursue your life goals.

As I write this section, I have been traveling for almost three weeks. It's July 4th, and my wife and I are at our little beach condo in Florida. My staff knows what to do. They don't need me. We were in Australia for almost two weeks, and I didn't have a phone with me. My wife asked me about ten days into the trip, "Have you talked to your office?" I said, "Uh, no." "Don't you need to check in with them?" she pressed. "Uh, no…they know what to do. Remember I have a turnkey business." "Oh that's right," she said.

One of my coaching clients built his business from almost nothing to over $2 million per year—and he takes fourteen vacation weeks each year and travels all around the world. It can be done. Now please understand that you don't want to be irresponsible. You still have a responsibility as the owner of that company. You must make sure that your managers are leading properly and that things are being implemented properly.

I liken it to investment property that is managed by someone else. You own the property (and therefore have responsibility), but you don't have to do the day-to-day management.

Another caution is not to exit too soon. I have another client who did not have the right team; and although his business was profitable and he was able to travel a great deal, he began to travel continuously and things began to fall into disrepair.

A saleable business

Finally, would you like to sell your business for a lot of money one of these days? What if one day you could sell your business and retire on the proceeds? How would that be? I have found that there are two responses to this question. The first one is, *"No! I love what I do!"* And the fact is that many times the work we do in our business is a ministry—it's our expression—or perhaps we love the technical work we do (or some other part of the work "in" the business).

If that is your response, you still need systems in your business! Here's why. What if you had to sell your business? A friend of mine has a hereditary kidney condition that will one day take his life. It took his brother's life. As far as he knows, it is inevitable.

The problem is that his current business depends on him! He is a genius at what he does, but it isn't a turnkey system. So, he has been feverishly building another company that will help him reach his most important life goal: to leave his family with the finances they need to live comfortably.

You may not want to sell your business right now. But sooner or later, you will "leave the building," as we all do! Whoever takes over that business will need a system. And if you have to sell it for some reason, you can.

The other response I get to the question "Would you like to sell your business for a lot of money one of these days?" is a resounding "YES!" Well, here's the bad news: first, your business isn't worth much if it depends on you. Second, an investor (someone who has the kind of money you probably want for your business) doesn't want your 24-hour-7-day-a-week JOB!

They want a set of keys.

They want a set of keys that they can take and turn the crank on the predictable, profitable, turnkey money machine that you have created. They want to be able to flip the ignition switch and have it run as good for them as it does for you.

✳✳✳

A friend of mine asked his billionaire neighbor (who owns a *lot* of companies) for advice. The billionaire business owner said, "Build your business to sell it and then keep it!"

If you are a skeptic, you may think it's a fantasy to have a turnkey business that allows you to travel and do the things you want to do. And you may be the type of business owner who believes you have to be there controlling every aspect of the business and that if you are off at the beach that your employees won't take you seriously.

To the skeptic: I'm living proof that it's possible. And I have helped many people do the same. It is possible. It won't be easy; in fact, building systems in your business will be the hardest thing you ever do in business. That's the bad news. The good news is that once you have a turnkey business, you will have something that very few small business owners have.

To the control freak: If you love running the thing every day and that fits your life goal, go for it! But if you think that is the only way, let me ask you this question. Is Warren Buffet on the floor of the call center at Geico? I don't think so. Phenomenal leadership is required to develop leaders who develop leaders. Leaders who can run your companies *for* you. Those who can handle the day to day *for* you and *instead* of you.

This acronym sums it up well:

Saves

Your

Self

Time

Energy

Money

Here's my acronym for SYSTEMS:

Systematizing

Your

Strategies

To

Execute

Management

Successfully

Everyone has strategies. You may not realize how many strategies you have, but you have specific ways of doing things. You may have intentionally decided to answer your phone a certain way rather than another, for example. That's a *strategy*. There's a certain way you do your work. That's a *strategy*. There's a certain way you advertise. That's a *strategy*.

A system is a group of working parts that are *designed* to work *together*. Then and only then can you really execute successfully. Then and only then can you really *manage*.

By the way, even if you are a solo operator or an independent professional who works alone, you need systems. There is a specific order of things that works best. Once you find the best procedure and timing, do it the same way each time and your results improve. Once you have tested a number of strategies, you find what works best and duplicate it over and over.

The Five Vital Components of a System

If you understand and apply the following components, you can systematize just about anything. Assembling these five components creates the ultimate system. I believe these five components will work for any type of business or organization:

1. The Mission

2. The Organizational Chart

3. Policies

4. Procedures

5. Job Descriptions

Systems Component #1: The Mission

Your company's mission is the unique experience you are delivering every day. It is what you do every day to accomplish the vision. Your mission is different from your vision. Your vision is where you are going. Your mission is how you get there.

For our purpose of learning together, we will define vision as being more about your goals, the destination, where we are going (remember GPS?). Your mission is about what you do every day.

For example, the mission of my service company is to provide the most outstanding service experience ever. The mission of my training company is to help small business owners stop being a slave to their business.

Starbucks's mission is *to inspire and nurture the human spirit - one person, one cup, and one neighborhood at a time.* World Famous Pike Place Fish Market became "world famous" by adopting the mission of *treating everyone like they're world famous.*

Notice that each of these statements is only one sentence and easy to remember. An effective mission statement is not some long boring paragraph in a frame on the wall that no one knows. The receptionist sitting ten feet away who sees it every day can't even tell you what is says. The owner who cooked it up in a business planning session with a consultant quickly forgot about it after the conference. Until you simplify it and transfer it into the hearts of your employees and clients, it won't help you.

Speaking of heart and the reason mission is the first component of building systems in your business, a system without a heart is just a lifeless corpse. If you think about the human body, as intricate as it is, without a heart pumping, there is no life. You can have the bones, the flesh, and all the intricate systems, but without blood flow, you have nothing.

Some organizations are alive, but that's about all. The next step is to make your mission inspirational. Your mission needs to be unique, meaningful, and engaging so that your employees feel good about delivering it and your clients get an experience that makes them feel good.

Whether you're a doctor or you sell a product online, what is the unique experience you want your clients, members, or patients to *feel?* A mission is not a slogan necessarily, it's what you actually *deliver.* But you *do* want to teach it to your clients so they know what they are getting. This helps you attract the kinds of clients you want. See more about that in the chapter on phenomenal marketing systems.

For example, the mission of my service company (to provide the most outstanding service experience ever) means we stand out from the crowd. Clients get a "wow" experience that makes them feel important. It makes them feel special. It makes them happy! Zappos created a phenomenal online business by making customers *happy!*

Instead of just providing a functional service, we offer an outstanding, engaging, meaningful service experience that leaves them with their jaws on the ground. Our goal is to leave them with the feeling that no one cares like we do. No one has *ever* provided that level of experience.

The first thing a new hire learns is our mission. In fact, they learn it in the interview process and agree to help us provide it before we even hire them. We have a five-page document on the mission that is the first part of the new hire training manual. It covers what the "most outstanding service experience ever" means. It not only talks about being on time and doing a good job, those kinds of things are blow the minimum standard.

The document teaches that success is only achieved when clients *feel* they have received *the most outstanding service experience* they have *ever* received from *any* service provider in any industry! It doesn't matter if we did everything we were "supposed" to do, we didn't accomplish the mission unless we can clearly see that they feel that way.

The Ritz-Carlton does a phenomenal job with this. They have a credo card that each one of their "Ladies and Gentlemen" carries. It has their credo, motto, and three steps of service on it. Read all about it in my friend Joseph Michelli's book, *The New Gold Standard.*

In my membership program, our mission is *to provide the most phenomenal community experience ever.* We found that when people feel like they belong to an organization that shares the same vision and values, they feel accepted, appreciated, and supported.

When they feel accepted, appreciated, and supported, they implement! The number one reason that small business owners don't grow is FTI (Failure To Implement)! We move them from being a slave to their business into a community of supporters, encouragers, and cheerleaders, and then on to implementation, infrastructure, and significant business growth.

The Benefits of a Clear, Compelling Mission

- *Your mission reveals who your target market is.* Does everyone want the most outstanding service experience? No, some people want the lowest price. Does everyone feel like a slave to their business? No. Does everyone want the finest coffee in the world? No. If you try to be everything to everyone, you won't be anything to anybody. (See the chapter on phenomenal marketing systems to see how mission affects marketing.)

- *Your mission dictates what kind of marketing you do.* Does every kind of marketing attract the target market that wants the mission you want to deliver? No.

- *Your mission engages your prospects and clients.* Your mission makes it clear what you are actually providing—an experience, not just a functional product or service.

- *Your mission helps your staff make the right client decisions.* This is possibly the biggest reason for a mission. Although your goal in building systems is to document every step that happens in the business, the fact is that we live in the real world and your staff must be empowered to make decisions when the lines are grey. How do your employees make that decision? With the mission in mind. Obviously we can't deliver the mission without making a profit (an important part of the vision), but the mission helps them make the right decision.

- *Your mission determines what image you project.* Your mission will determine how your materials look, what kind of dress code you have, what kind of facility you have, and many other decisions regarding the image of your company. For example, if my target market is corporate America, my image has to be corporate. If my target market is small business owners, it can be a little more down to earth, as they want to see authenticity.

- *Your mission helps you adopt the right customer service policies.* One of the biggest disconnects in small business is when the mission doesn't match the message. If the message says you provide the most outstanding service experience ever, but you set policies that limit your staff from actually delivering that, you hurt the brand.

- *Your mission leads you to the right procedures and training processes.* Your people can have hearts as big as Texas, but if they don't have the training and the systems to work with, they can't deliver even if they wanted to.

- *Your mission tells you what kind of people you should hire (or not).* If your people aren't passionate about the mission, you are going nowhere fast. As Jim Collins says in *Good to Great,* "Get the right people on the bus and then figure out what seat to put them in." (More about this in Phenomenal Leadership Systems.)

- *Your mission is the focus of coaching and discipline.* When team members miss the mark and you have to take them into a coaching situation, the entire conversation is about mission, vision, and purpose. This takes the conversation away from "me versus you." It's about the mission. This takes the negative emotion out of the equation.

Once you have a mission that you believe in, you can use it to make every decision in your business. What kind of marketing should we do? What should our uniforms look like? What kind of equipment should we use? In the book *Onward,* Howard Shultz shares that when Starbucks got off-track, the espresso machines that were chosen to cut expenses actually killed part of the experience—the aroma!

You can be tempted to do things that keep you from accomplishing your mission because you are trying to save money or you're growing so fast that you lose sight of what got you there in the first place. That's what happened to Starbucks.

In the book *Onward—How Starbucks Fought for Its Life without Losing Its Soul,* Howard Shultz shares how they regained their brand after losing their way. It's a powerful story about the importance of mission and brand.

When you have a mission that is understood, you can "check" every decision that is made. A clear mission helps you "rally the troops" and gives you a context for coaching. When an employee doesn't follow procedure, you can simply tie the correct behavior to the "why" behind the procedure—which is the mission.

Instead of your employees thinking you're mad at them or you don't like them or whatever emotional issue they have, they understand that it's about the mission. They understand that the mission is best for the client. Speaking of clients, be sure to communicate your mission to your prospects, customers, and clients, as well. At our company, our UEP™ (Unique Experience Proposition) is our mission statement. This is what the client is buying and this is what my staff provides.

What a thing of beauty!

The mission is the very first component in building systems because we must know what it is that we are trying to accomplish each day. While you are getting your procedures in place, your team needs to know what the mission is so they can make the right decisions. You also need your mission in place so you can create the right procedures.

As mentioned previously, you may have heard people use the words "vision" and "mission" interchangeably. The difference between vision and mission, by the way (in my mind's eye), is this:

Mission is what your business is trying to *do* each day. In other words, every time we pick up the phone, it communicates "the most outstanding service experience ever"—or it doesn't. Simple as that.

Vision is what you want your business to *look* like. In other words, your vision is what you get when you reach your goals. We want to do X number of dollars in business, X number of clients, X dollars in profit, etc. We want to have X number of trucks, staff, etc.

Finally, your mission is supported by your *values* or what Starbucks calls "guiding principles." These values help us live out our mission each day. My company has five values that we live by and that we communicate to our clients.

If we live out the values, we accomplish the mission. Simple as that.

To create your own mission statement, think about what you want the client to receive. What do you want them to *feel?* Put together a simple but meaningful sentence and begin to communicate it to your staff. Post it on your materials, your walls, and every place it can be visible to remind you, your staff, and your clients what you are actually selling.

Systems Component #2: The Organizational Chart

Owning your own business can be overwhelming because of the number of "hats" you have to wear. Someone not only has to do the technical work of the business, but someone has to market, someone has to go on sales calls, someone has to do the bookkeeping, someone has to order supplies, someone has to fix the equipment, and the list goes on.

If you are a larger company and you have people actually doing some of these things, you are most likely overwhelmed as you try to manage them and end up being involved in many things that you don't want to be involved in (and probably shouldn't be).

You are involved in too many areas because you haven't learned the skill of leadership and systems. How do you ever get past this? You need a vision. A road map—a clear picture of the business. A great tool is an organizational chart.

An organizational chart for most companies looks like this:

LEADERSHIP	MARKETING	SALES	OPERATIONS	ADMINISTRATION
Directing	You	You	You	You
Managing	You	You	You	You
Doing	You	You	You	You

No wonder you're overwhelmed! You're in every box!

So how do you get organized? You begin by understanding the 12 vital functions of the business. Every one of these functions is vital to becoming phenomenally successful in your business. And if you want a turnkey business, all of them are absolutely crucial.

Does someone have to plan the business to be more successful? You bet. That's the role of the person I call the Director. Does someone have to manage the business? Absolutely. Someone must make sure that all of the things that are supposed to happen actually get implemented. I call that person the Manager.

And, of course, someone has to actually do the work of the business. The good news is that it doesn't always have to be you. And men, your wife is not the only one who can answer the phone and do the books. She needs a life, too.

Understanding the three levels of leadership (directing, managing, and doing) gives you a picture of how to separate and organize the major functions. Then there are what I call the Four Pillars of a Phenomenally Successful Business: *Marketing* (everything you do to attract prospects to your business), *Sales* (everything you do to convert the prospect into paying customer), *Operations* (everything you do to service your client), and *Administration* (everything you do to track results).

More on these areas in the next chapter.

How to Use the Organizational Chart

1. *Directing* is casting the vision for the company, planning, and leading the managers. The director knows what the end result looks like.

2. *Managing* ensures that the wishes of the director are carried out. This involves training, supervising, reporting, and overseeing resources.

3. *Doing* is implementing the work to be done.

To grow effectively, begin replacing yourself in the "doing" area on the bottom row first. As a business owner, your time is worth more than $15 per hour. When you begin to grow, replace yourself in those areas first. Start with the area you are not good at. Stay in your strength zone.

For example, if you're good at marketing but hate bookkeeping, the Administration area is probably suffering. Get a clerk or a bookkeeper who can help in that area. Or perhaps you don't like doing the technical work of the business (or that is the most overwhelming, time consuming area for you). Put someone in place to do the basic parts of Operations so you can focus on Marketing, Sales, and Administration.

When I started my first company out of the trunk of my car, my name was in every box just like this chart. Of course at that time I didn't even know there *were* boxes! Eventually I hired an operations assistant. Then I hired a couple of operations technicians. Then I hired people to answer the phone (inside sales), to send out newsletters and marketing materials, and to do data entry (Administration). I hired a bookkeeper. I did the marketing and outside sales.

Later on I merged with a couple of other small business owners and put one in charge of Operations and the other in charge of Administration. We then hired more people to do inside sales and on-location sales. Eventually, I hired someone to do marketing *with* me and then *for* me.

Finally I was only in two boxes—Marketing Director and Sales Director. Today my business is turnkey. Although I meet with my staff once a week and we work on projects, I don't really have a "job" in that business other than the responsibility of owning the business.

Once you fill the bottom boxes, you can move to the middle boxes. In fact, it doesn't even have to be that clean. You may still be "doing" some of the work while having managers in other areas. For example, as I write this book, I am "doing" work "in" the business. At the time of this writing, I present workshops, seminars, and do some coaching and consulting in addition to writing, but I have an Operations Manager, a Marketing Manager, Sales Manager, and an Administration Manager.

Although I'm doing some work "in" the business, it is strategic work that I enjoy doing—work that reaps big rewards. However, if at any point I want to stop doing any part of what I do "in" the business, I can. When you build it with systems in mind, you create something that can survive and thrive beyond you.

The Four Roles of the Business Owner

On the Wheel of Life, mentioned in Chapter 1, there's a spoke called "Career." You want to think about what *role* you want to fulfill in your small business. Don't worry about *how* right now. Just think about your life goals and what kind of work lifestyle you are after. Remember that you want to design your business around your life goals. There are four roles you can choose to fulfill in your small business.

1. *The Technician.* What I mean by technician is the one doing the technical work of the business. In a service business, the technician role is obvious, but even if you run a retail store or you are an independent professional, the doing of the work is who I am talking about—the person making the sales calls, processing paperwork, or serving customers. It is the *doing* of the work.

   Is there anything wrong with being the technician in your business? Absolutely not! If that's what you truly love to do—if that's what you are called to do—and you can balance your life, it may be a wonderful thing for you. You may want to do what doctors do—put in place an administrative staff and assistants so you can grow your "practice." All of the concepts in this chapter will assist you, even if you want to continue doing the technical work. But you must organize the other aspects of the business so you are not so overwhelmed. I want you to be the technician because you *want* to, not because you feel you *have* to!

2. *The Customer Service Manager.* This level is when you have others doing the majority of the technical work, but you are still managing the service experience. A good example of this is an in-home

service company. Say you are a plumber and you are normally the one who does the work. Once you develop a system, even an ordinary plumber can get extraordinary results by simply using the system that you have developed. You are still "controlling" the client experience by directing the action. You talk to the client over the phone and sometimes stop in to check on the job's progress.

3. *The General Manager.* At this level, you have a team that does most of the day-to-day duties—marketing, sales, service, and accounting. But you are there to direct the operation. Sure you can take a vacation and leave someone in charge, but you call the day-to-day shots.

4. *The Turnkey Business Owner.* This is a level I think all business owners dream of, but, sadly, few ever reach. You have management in place that call the day-to-day shots. You can do what you want to do, when you want to do it. If you want to go away for the summer, you can. Some people believe this is a fantasy. Of course, I'm living proof that this can be done—and I've helped others do it too.

But let's look at some examples that maybe you can relate to—Walmart and Sam's Club. Could Sam Walton be in every store? No. He loved to be involved where he could, but it was impossible for him to be involved in everything that happened at Sam's and Walmart. "But Howard, that's a *huge* company. What does that have to do with me?" you might ask. *At one time, Sam Walton had **one** store!*

What about Warren Buffet? Does he answer the phone at Geico and write insurance? No. Does he work the floor at the Omaha-based furniture store that he owns? Of course not. So the point here is that you have to start somewhere. And the place you want to start is getting your business systematized and organized so it is more predictable. You want to begin the process of replacing yourself in the areas that you are not good at and that you are not supposed to do.

Systems Component #3: Policies

These are the guidelines—the rules and regulations. Policies are to clarify expectations on conduct issues, dress code, etc. A good example of a set of policies is what would be in your Employee Handbook.

Be sure that your policies complement your mission rather than compete with it. For instance, if your mission is to provide the most outstanding service experience ever, don't make policies that are going to frustrate the clients.

You can get an Employee Handbook template for your state. Make any needed changes to it and have a labor attorney review it. The technical policies for your industry may be found through industry associations, etc. Otherwise, you'll have to write them line by line. Even if you get something that is already "complete", chances are that you'll have to invest some time tweaking it.

Systems Component #4: Procedures

A procedure is the "how to." Make your procedures step by step. If it is a computer program, include each keystroke (within reason, you can't always cover every possibility). If your industry has technical training or manuals to use, you can cut the development time down. We have one department in one of my companies where a technical manual developed by a training company in our industry is used as our technical manual. Whatever the book says, that's how we do it.

The idea is that someone who has never done the work can follow the procedure and can do it without any further instructions. This reminds me of when I first started traveling to present workshops. My brother was traveling with me because he has an accounting business that requires only a few months of his time, and he's basically "off" the rest of the year. We were on an airplane and he was sitting behind me.

I simply handed the timeline and procedure for the one-day workshop over the back of the seat, and he read it on the plane. The next morning when I stopped the workshop for a break, I couldn't find my brother! The rental car was gone and so was he! *Where could he have possibly gone?* I thought to myself. A few minutes later, he walked in with a Starbucks in his hand.

You're kidding! I'm thinking to myself. Here we are on break and I need help with orders, and he's at Starbucks! "Why did you go to Starbucks?" I asked him. "Because the procedure said to go get you a coffee from Starbucks during the break and to be back by 10:30. Two sugars right?" he said. I had taken the break a few minutes early. He followed the procedure. I didn't!

Although that's kind of a funny story, it proves how you can write a procedure, hand it off, and not worry about it.

Systems Component #5: Position Results Descriptions

Once you've determined what positions you are going to fulfill in the business, you need to fill in the other boxes. Position descriptions or job descriptions is the next component. Position descriptions outline each of the roles and the duties required to fulfill that position.

Many job description examples are long and cumbersome. A simple way to do it is to create a line item for each position. Each of the items will be connected to a policy or procedure. Each of these line items can also be called a Key Result Area (KRA). A KRA spells out the results that are expected for each key area. For example, a bookkeeper position description would have a KRA called Accounts Payable. It would read as follows:

Key Result Area: Accounts Payable. My job in this area will have been completed when I have entered all payables according to our company Accounts Payable Policies and Procedures.

The task is connected to a policy or procedure. It may have been done, but done wrong. Attaching the KRA to a policy or procedure ensures it was done right, but does not require you to write every policy or procedure before you can create position descriptions.

Start with a simple checklist of Key Result Areas, then add the Policies and Procedures as you create them.

Three Simple Brain-Dead Steps to Get Started Building Systems Now

Step 1: Make a long list of "tasks" or procedures. Think of everything that happens in your company. Keep adding to the list until you have the major Key Result Areas (KRA) identified.

Step 2: Assign the KRAs to a specific person in a position description. Discuss the position description with the team member.

Step 3: Begin developing your most important policies and procedures. Communicate them in writing and in training to your team.

Bookkeeper

My job in the following areas will be completed when I have:

1. Entered all job tickets according to the Job Ticket Entering Procedure

2. Entered all incoming bills according to the Accounts Payable Procedures

3. Invoiced all unpaid accounts according to the Accounts Receivable Procedures

4. Made the Bank Deposit according to the Bank Deposit Procedure

5. Sent out all Referral Certificates according to the Referral Certificate Procedures

Job Description Checklist

Daily

- ☐ Process Incoming E-Mail
- ☐ Post on Social Media
- ☐ Make 20 Referral Calls

Weekly

- ☐ Send Weekly E-Mail Newsletter
- ☐ Attend Weekly Staff Meeting
- ☐ Submit Weekly Marketing Report
- ☐ Change All Banner Ads
- ☐ Update Websites

Monthly

- ☐ Send Monthly Newsletter
- ☐ Update Print Ads
- ☐ Update Marketing Plan
- ☐ Submit Magazine Article

Chapter 4

The Five Secrets of a Phenomenal Business

"The secret is the system." –Michael E. Gerber

In 2011, I had the pleasure of helping Tom Ziglar, son of Zig Ziglar, create a powerful business assessment for Zig Ziglar's last book *Born To Win*, which Tom co-authored. Tom and I had our own lists of the core systems a business should have, and they were a little different. As we began to flesh out the parts that every phenomenally successful business needs to have, we finally settled on five specific areas of the business.

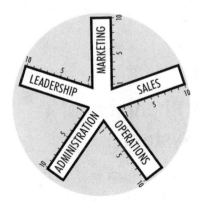

Secret #1: A Phenomenal Marketing System

Marketing is everything you do to attract *prospects* to your business. Notice that I said a *phenomenal* marketing *system*. The marketing of most small business owners is poor.

Marketing is the key to business growth. Without customers you have nothing. You can do a wonderful job, but if you don't have enough customers, nothing else matters. So, you want to have not just good marketing, but phenomenal marketing. What is phenomenal marketing? Marketing that is remarkable. Extraordinary. Outstanding. Phenomenal marketing creates experiences that engage, educate, and build a sense of belonging.

And you want to have a marketing *system*. Once you determine what phenomenal marketing looks like in your business, you want to figure out how to duplicate it without you having to be involved in every detail.

Here's an example: Let's say that you determine that mailing a newsletter to your database helps you bring in more business. You write a procedure on how to compile the newsletter and get someone else to do the mechanics of it. You might still write it, but let someone else lay it out, print it, mail it, get the database together, etc. Then put the task on a calendar so it happens without your direct supervision.

This book reveals the proven secrets of a phenomenal marketing system that has revolutionized small businesses worldwide.

Secret #2: A Phenomenal Sales System

"Sales" is everything you do to turn a prospect into a paying *customer*. Once you generate prospects through marketing, the sales system is what turns them from prospects to customers. Remember, you want a *phenomenal* sales *system*.

This system includes answering the phone, your phone scripts, responding to an email opt-in, presentations, and so on. Once they have actually purchased something from you, they are now customers.

Many times you may not need more prospects, but you need to take better care of the leads you get. Is your phone answered live? Is your phone answered in the most professional way possible? Do prospects and clients have a great experience when they call your company? Are your closing ratios what they need to be? Do you consistently make the add-on sale?

Do you have proven scripts for your people to follow so that you aren't the only one who can close the "big deals"? Do you have phenomenal on-site sales materials? How effective is your response to Internet leads? Increasing your closing ratios and your job averages can have a big impact on your business.

This book shows you my proven sales system for building a phenomenal business.

Secret #3: A Phenomenal Operations System

Operations is everything you do to service your customer, patient, or member. The level of service you provide determines whether they will ascend the "loyalty ladder" and go from customer to *client*. What's the difference between a customer and a client? A customer buys something solely on the price, value, or special, but doesn't have any loyalty to you. A client wants a consultant, an advisor, or a partner, so to speak, to "take care of that area of their lives."

You wouldn't choose a doctor based on price, would you? Or how about finding the cheapest accountant or attorney? If you do, you'll get what you pay for. Clients are loyal, they want a relationship, they want information, and they refer others like them.

Do you have service systems in place so that your clients get *the* most phenomenal service experience *ever*, consistently *every* time? Without you having to be personally involved?

In this book, you'll learn how to take this area to the next level.

Secret #4: A Phenomenal Administration System

Administration is tracking results. It is also internal office systems that include financial, accounting, legal, insurance, and those types of things.

Do you know what your cost of doing business is? Do you know what your marketing efforts are producing? Do you know what your sales closing rates are? Do you know what your production rates are? Do you have a budget for the next 12 months? Do you have the right insurance and legal protection?

I think I just felt you become overwhelmed with all the "work" you have to do. Let me pause for a moment and take you back to Chapter 1: The *One* and *Only* Reason Your Business Exists…to Be a Vehicle to Help You Achieve Your LIFE Goals.

If you want to build a predictable, profitable, turnkey vehicle that will take you where you want to go in life, it will be a lot of work to build it. But it will be worth it.

Can you imagine a 747 flying across the ocean without knowing stats? Without knowing what the fuel level is? Yet, this is what small businesses do every day. They guess. They don't track. This is one of the most important parts of your business.

If you don't make money, your business isn't working! A business without a profit is just a *hobby!* And the only way you know whether you are making a profit is to track.

Tracking helps you make more while working less.

Read that sentence again. Tracking will help you work less and make more. Why? Because when you get in touch with your *actual* numbers (prepare to be surprised), it will cause you to stop running harder on the hamster wheel and take action on the things that actually matter.

You will not only get an education on this subject in this book, but you'll also learn a *phenomenal* administration *system*.

Secret #5: A Phenomenal Leadership System

In 2011, I had the opportunity to meet John Maxwell, the world's number one leadership expert. As the first person to become a founding member of John's very first coaching program *The John Maxwell Team*, I had the opportunity to spend time with John. The highlight was watching the Super Bowl at his home in Florida.

John says, "Everything rises and falls on leadership." *Everything?* Can that be true? He goes on to say that "leadership is influence." Nothing more, nothing less. And to gain influence, you must "add value to people." Is leadership required for marketing? Only if you want to influence people to do business with your company. And remember that all of business is about *relationships*. Marketing, sales, and service is about relationships. Tracking your numbers reflects your relationship with yourself! Are you serious about your life goals? Or are you using your business just to get by in life? To have something to do?

Speaking of this, John Maxwell also says the toughest person to lead is yourself. When you begin to understand your strengths and weaknesses, and you begin to understand how to add value to other people—to influence them and to "enlist their willing cooperation to reach a goal" (Dale Carnegie)—you can begin to build a phenomenal team.

This means that you don't have to do everything yourself. It means you can now find those people who can do the things you don't like to do (and probably aren't very good at). My strengths are marketing, sales, service, and leadership. Did you notice that administration wasn't listed? I hated the numbers! Until I got in trouble. Then I began to love the fact that I could predict a loss in the future and do something about it before it happened!

I have a staff of forty people who run my companies for me. I can tell you without hesitation that one of my greatest joys in life is watching my team grow. To watch my managers grow as leaders (there is a difference you know), is thrilling.

The reason it is thrilling is because we now have a *phenomenal* leadership *system*.

This book reveals how you can have one too!

Free Audio Program Reveals the 5 Secrets

This Audio Program was recorded by Howard Partridge and
Tom Ziglar at the legendary Zig Ziglar studio.

Chapter 5

Phenomenal Marketing Systems

What comes to mind when you think of the word *marketing?* For some, it's advertising. Others might think of networking, branding, or the idea of "getting your name out there."

Of course marketing includes those things, but marketing is actually *everything* you do to *attract prospects* to your business. *Phenomenal* marketing delivers a meaningful *experience* that educates, engages, and entertains. A phenomenal marketing *system* is a group of working parts that *duplicates results* consistently.

What kind of results? Enough of your perfect target prospects to reach your sales goal consistently. A phenomenal marketing system consistently produces your perfect target prospect. If you are attracting the wrong kind of prospect, your marketing isn't working. And if your sales are up and down because you don't consistently implement marketing, then you don't have a system. Too many business owners spend lots of time and money "getting their name out there" but have no real system of attracting prospects consistently. Most often, a small business owner's marketing is a gamble more than a planned effort. Congratulations for reading this book. You now have the opportunity to be one of the few who escape that trap.

Regardless of the type of marketing you do, it must *increase sales*. Of course the sales process will determine whether the prospect will actually buy, but that also depends on the quality of the prospect you are attracting. When you attract the wrong kind of customer (because your marketing isn't what it needs to be), it doesn't matter how good your sales process is. You may even close the sale, but you won't build the kind of business you want.

The Only Three Ways to Increase Sales

Regardless of the type of business you are in, there are only three ways to increase sales under the sun. The three ways are:

1. Increase Sales from Existing Clients.

The first (and possibly the easiest) way to increase sales is to get your existing clients to use your services (or buy your product) more often, or to use more of your services (or buy more of your products). This can have a dramatic effect on your income. If you are not marketing to your existing client base, you could literally double your business with this strategy alone. This is assuming that you have something compelling and valuable to offer your past and existing clients.

As you'll see, marketing to your past and existing clients is one of the most important marketing activities. In fact, not marketing to your past clients is what I call "The Biggest Marketing Mistake of ALL," but we'll get to that.

It is estimated that it costs an average of 500 percent more to gain a new client than to keep an existing one. They already know you. You already know them. They have already paid your price. They are the most likely to do business with you assuming that you have a repeatable service, other products, and you want referrals from them.

Later on I share the reasons this is one of the biggest secrets. This book reveals some of the strategies you can use to keep your current clients coming back for more and to keep them actively referring you.

2. Increase Number of Clients.

Speaking of referrals, the second way to increase sales is to get more clients. This is the one that people usually think of first. Most small business owners say that 85 percent of their business comes from repeat and referral business. Yet they don't have a system in place to maintain and increase repeat and referral business. Most small business owners say they build their business through "word of mouth," but they don't have a referral *system* in place. There are many ways to get more clients, but the best way is through referrals, and I'll show you how to put your word of mouth marketing into a phenomenal system.

3. Increase Price.

This is a powerful way to increase sales, but probably the last one that small business owners think of. In fact, you only think of it briefly, because after all, "With the economy being what it is…." I hope to change your mind on this, because when you increase your price without losing too much in sales volume, your top line increases. If you raise your price 20 percent and lose 20 percent of your sales volume, you are still making more profit. If you raise your price 50 percent and lose 50 percent of your sales volume, you are still making more profit.

By positioning yourself and your company differently—by creating a different message—you will be able to continually raise your price. The beauty is that you probably *won't* lose any sales volume! If you do lose clients, it'll be the unprofitable ones you don't want anyway. And if you do this right, you'll quickly replace them with clients who are willing to pay a higher price because you will have developed a compelling experience they want to have.

Experiential Marketing

Speaking of experience, I came across a term some years ago that explained what I was already doing in my marketing, and explained how I was able to get the highest prices. The term "experiential marketing" is sort of an unusual, obscure term, but is key to getting the highest prices for your service. In his book *Experiential Marketing*, Bernd H. Schmitt states:

> Today, customers take functional features and benefits, product quality, and a positive brand image as a given. What they want is products, communications, and marketing campaigns that dazzle their senses, touch their hearts and stimulate their minds. They want products communications and campaigns that they can relate to and that they can incorporate into their lifestyles. The want products, communications, and marketing campaigns to deliver an experience…

Notice that it says to deliver an experience in the *marketing campaign*. Hopefully all of us know that we must create the most unique and powerful experience when we actually serve our clients. But what this is saying is that it is created in the marketing campaign. Interesting.

The quote goes on to say:

> The degree to which a company is able to deliver a desirable customer experience (in the marketing) and to use information technology, brands, and integrated communications and entertainment to do so, will largely determine its success in the global marketplace of the new millennium.

You may not be concerned about the "global marketplace" in your industry, but the degree to which we understand and implement this concept determines the degree of success we will have in getting higher prices.

What is the marketing message of most business owners? How do average, everyday businesses advertise their services? If your industry is like most, you will find that the message is either about price or about how they do their work. If you sell a product, it's all about the features of the product.

Let's deal with price advertising first. Price advertising comes in many different ways. The most common type of price advertising is placing an ad that offers a low price. But that's not the only type of price advertising. The way that you carry yourself as the business owner is a reflection of the value of your service experience.

How you dress, what your company materials look like, what your office looks like, how you answer your telephone, etc. You see, you *will* take up a position in the marketplace, just by existing. The question is whether you will take up the position that you *want* or not. You have to *design* and create your position, rather than letting it happen by accident.

Avoiding the Three Types of "Price Advertising"

One of the worst things you can do in marketing is advertise *price* before *value* is proven. The most common type of price advertiser is the one that advertises a ridiculously low price never intending to honor that price. Or, they have one in stock at that price. In the worst cases, you could categorize these price advertisers in the "bait n' switch" category. They bait the prospect with a low price to get in the door. Once the prospect is generated, they switch them to what they really want to sell. In the worst cases, the company would even refuse to offer the low price service. Do you have bait n' switch operators in your industry?

The *bait n' switch advertiser is only one* of **three types of price advertisers**. The *second is what I call the "value choice."* The value choice, unlike the bait n' switch is a legitimate business model, but has intentionally positioned itself as the lower price alternative. Think of how Southwest Airlines started.

They intentionally positioned themselves as the low price alternative and they were very focused about running their business model accordingly.

Not offering meals on their flights, their point-to-point routes, open seating, and the revolutionary "10 minute turn around" have all kept their costs low so they can offer a lower price and make a healthy profit. This model doesn't work for the small business that doesn't have the scope or infrastructure that a large company has.

This brings me to the third type of price advertiser. *The third type of price advertiser is the small business that doesn't have the management infrastructure, the reach, and cannot handle the volume that a larger company can.* Let's think about a plumbing company. If a plumber is a smaller operator, why would he want to match the price of a bigger operation?

He can't compete with their margins. He doesn't have the management infrastructure, the capital, the brand image, and the television commercials that the larger company has. His revenue is generated by his sweat. Therefore, even though the overhead is lower, this person should charge more, rather than less. The key is that this plumber must understand what differentiates him from the larger firm, which we will get to in a moment.

But, let's look at a comparison between the smaller operator and the larger company. Let's say this is the income statement of the larger firm:

$5M Income

- $2.5M Cost of Sale

=$2.5 M Gross Profit

- $2.0M Fixed Expense (40%)

=$500k Net Income

If a smaller operator who billed $200,000 has the same cost structure that produces a 10 percent margin, he would end up with $20,000 in profit. Not cool! And that's what is happening in small businesses around the world every day! Obviously there are lots of variables in this scenario, but the point is that you can't compete with the larger company on price.

Instead, the smaller operator should charge higher prices and leverage the benefits that a smaller operator can offer. So the saddest case of all the price advertisers are the small, independent business owners who just copy the big company instead of understanding how to position themselves differently.

The bottom line is that price advertising attracts price shoppers. So don't do that!

The Effects of Lowering or Raising Price

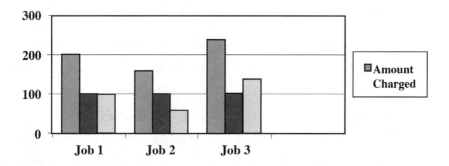

In this simplified illustration, Job 1 (which could be Product 1) is priced at $200 and the cost of producing it is $100, which would give you a $100 profit.

Job 2 offers a discount of 20 percent, which would make the price $160. Guess what doesn't change? The cost! It still costs $100 to do that job! So that means your profit went down to $60.

That's a 40 percent drop!

What if you could position your company in a way that you could charge 20 percent more instead of less? What do you think would happen?

Let's take a look…

Job 3 is priced at $240 instead of $200. What stays the same? The cost! $240 minus $100 gives us $140 *profit*. And by the way, *the difference in profit from Job 2 and Job 3 is 2.33 times the amount.*

That means you could do *half the work and make more money!*

Or do the same volume and make more than twice the money. This is a very important concept for smaller companies to understand. It's not in the volume (with any company), it's in the profit. It is terribly important as independent business owners to understand this because we don't have a national brand to generate leads for us. We have an entirely different set of benefits to offer, which are worth far more.

How They Do Their Work

The second way that most small business owners advertise their company is "how they do their work." Other than price, what could possibly be wrong with this? Let's look and see…

Let's say that Sue Smith is a CPA. When Sue introduces herself at a networking group, it will usually sound something like this, "Hi, I'm Sue Smith with 1-2-3 Accounting Firm and we do taxes. If you need anything to do with taxes, just give us a call. We do everything from soup to nuts, A to Z, you name it, we can do it. If you need anything, just gimme a call."

Isn't it true that just about every time you hear someone introduce themselves or you see an advertisement for a company *nothing* stands out that makes them unique and different?

The problem is that everyone is saying the same thing. So if you do the same thing, why should people choose you over another company? Why should they pay you a higher price? They shouldn't. This big mistake is repeated over and over by small business owners worldwide every single day. In today's competitive marketplace, it is not enough to just tell what you do or to tell the features and benefits of what you do.

How to Dominate Your Market and Get Rich in the Niche!

"If you try to be everything to everyone, you won't be anything to anyone!"

If you want to dominate a niche, you first have to know what your niche is. Do you know that when you try to be "everything" to everyone, you won't be "anything" to anyone? You want to be a BIG FISH in a small pond, rather than a minnow in a huge ocean. So, who is your perfect target niche client?

My good friend and business consultant Ellen Rohr explains a simple way to find out. Think about your very best customers. You know them—they never complain about price, they always pay on time, and they are a pleasure to work with. That picture describes your target niche market. Of course in your phenomenal marketing plan, you will determine the demographics (age, gender, income, etc.) and psychographics (purchasing habits, etc.) of your perfect target market.

Domination is a result of positioning.

In the classic marketing book *Positioning* by Jack Trout and Al Ries, they describe positioning as a slot in your target market's mind much like a file in a file cabinet. To illustrate this, let me ask you a couple of questions: When I say *laundry detergent*, what brand first comes to mind? For most it's

Tide. When I say *soft drink*, what brand comes to mind first? Most would say Coke.

Regardless of what brand comes to your mind, the one that did is the one that occupies that slot—the file in the file cabinet of your mind. So your job as a *phenomenal* marketer is to have a *system* for positioning yourself at the highest place in the mind of your perfect target market.

Positioning and domination is a result of being UNIQUE.

Let's look at three companies that have done this well:

1. *Whole Foods*—they recognized the growing trend of natural food enthusiasts (target market) and decided to take up a position in that space.

2. *Starbucks*—They created a unique experience around coffee—a commodity that has been around for thousands of years.

3. *Harley-Davidson*—Whether you're a biker or not, you must agree that there's a unique experience around owning and riding a hog! That could be good or bad depending on your view! LOL!

Being unique means you can charge more.

Why do you need to charge more? Because working 24/7 just to barely scrape by is not a phenomenal life. Remember, the only reason your business exists is to help you achieve your life goals. Why doesn't the *average* person shop at Whole Foods? Because of "cost." I personally love to shop at Whole Foods when I am home because they offer the natural foods that I want. I pay more, but I get what I want all at the same place. My wife points out that I could get certain items cheaper at other places, but I'm not interested in going to three different stores to get what I need, and none of the other stores have the natural food selection that I want.

How much can you spend on a cup of coffee at Starbucks?

I decided to find out, so I conducted an informal marketing survey. As I traveled around the country, I would go into Starbucks, walk up to the counter and say, "I want to buy your most expensive cup of coffee." Almost always without hesitation (but with a curious look on their faces), they would typically offer a Venti Salted Mocha Frappuccino or something like that. "How much is that?" I asked. "$6.25," they responded.

Then I say, "Can you make it more expensive?"

"What do you mean?" they ask.

"I want to buy the most expensive coffee I can," I insist. "For example, could you add some shots?"

"Sure."

"How many can you add?"

"As many as you want."

"Yeah, but the Venti cup only holds a certain amount, right?"

"Right."

So, they figure that up. Then almost without fail, another employee comes along and says "You could add some flavors." They are quick to remind me that I won't be able to drink it and I assure them that's okay because I don't want to drink it, I just want to get the most expensive cup of coffee I can find.

The highest price I have been able to find so far is $43.27!

Don't worry, I didn't pay that. In fact each episode ends the same way, "Never mind, I'll just have a tall cappuccino." They didn't laugh either. But I do always gave them a big tip for playing along, and they liked that. I recently came across a video of a guy who did the same experiment with Starbucks. He created a great video of the interaction and the actual sales receipt!

Harley-Davidson isn't concerned about being the cheapest bike around, right? They have created such an experience around their brand that people are willing to pay a high price to own one. Recently we held a leadership retreat in Colorado Springs, and a couple who are in our coaching program rode their Harley all the way from Florida. They built a 17-day vacation around the event. I went outside to see their bike, and the husband was beaming as he showed it off. It had a nice trailer, and he explained how it was top-of-the-line and how it had all the bells and whistles.

"How much you got in this bike?" I asked. "Sixty-five grand," he responded. He explained that the trailer had to be custom painted to match the bike and so on.

The Experience Economy

To demonstrate how this works, let me share a concept from a phenomenal book called *The Experience Economy* by Joe Pine and James Gilmore. What I learned from that book is when coffee first hits the market as a *commodity,* it costs about $1 a pound. Not much differentiation at this point other than the type of bean. Once it is packaged and appears on the shelf at the grocery store, it becomes a *good.*

How much does a pound of coffee cost at the grocery store? Having presented this message thousands of times, I have found that very few people know how much they pay for a cup of coffee! We just enter the store like zombies and grab our brand. LOL!

Coffee in the grocery store can range from $2.99 per pound (it's actually 12 ounces of coffee and 4 ounces of air—kind of like potato chips these days!), on up to more than ten bucks a pound. Now, we have gone from one dollar a pound to *three to ten times the price!*

For what? Packaging. The brand.

How is *your* packaging? How is *your* brand? Most small business owners are at the forefront of their businesses. Did you know that the way you dress, the way you carry yourself and the way you communicate *assigns* a value to you and your business?

The next level is the *service* level. If you go to Denny's and buy a cup of coffee, what are you really paying for? You're not really paying for coffee right? You are paying for the *service* of someone to brew that coffee and make it available to you.

How much does a cup of coffee cost at Denny's? About $1 per cup. How much of that *weak* coffee can you make from a pound of coffee? About 60 cups! So the price per pound goes up to about $60 a pound at Denny's.

When you think about your marketing message, are you talking enough about your unique service? When you sell the benefits of a unique service rather than just the work you do or the product features, you begin to set yourself apart and can therefore charge more than the commodity price.

How to get people to stand in line and pay you the highest prices for your product or service.

Finally, the next level is the *experience*. This would be having a cappuccino in Italy outside one of the historical landmarks. When we were there eight years ago, it was about $8 a cup. Another example of the experience level would be Starbucks. People stand in line to pay the highest prices for a cup of coffee—a commodity that has been around for thousands of years.

I have a picture I took in the Baltimore airport. There were 63 people standing in line at Starbucks. And that was just in a few minutes time. There were hundreds of people that stood in that line. Now here's a little disclaimer: the other two coffee places in that area were closed. But that's a message by itself. Why were they closed? I can only assume that management felt there weren't enough flights going out at that time to justify running the lights, and I can just hear them say that their employees don't like coming in that early anyway!

But Starbucks understands something the other coffee places don't. They understand that those 63 people are going to walk onto an airplane with hundreds of other people on it with something very important in their hands—not just a cup of coffee, but the logo on the cup. The brand. As each person sitting on that airplane sees that logo, it makes them wish they stood in line for it. They might be thinking, *I'm going to attack that man and take that cup of coffee!*

Now the question becomes "Can you do this in your small business?" And the answer is yes you can. Here's how.

The Phenomenal Five Point "Experiential" Marketing Message

Several years ago I developed my five point marketing message. This message covers what I believe are the five things that people will stand in line and pay the highest price for. When you have all five of them in place *and* you understand how to use them in your marketing, you can literally position yourself at the top of any industry. I've done it in three different industries and helped thousands of small business owners around the world in many different industries improve their position at minimum, and many have dominated their markets.

Here are the five points:

1. *Reputation.* There is one primary "unspoken" question that every prospect has about every person or company they do business with. Can you think of what it is? "Can I trust you?" is the question. They may not verbalize it just like that, but that is their number one question. So in your marketing message, you must

not only demonstrate *trust*, but *prove* that you have a phenomenal reputation.

2. *Experience.* The second unspoken question all prospects have about your business is "Do you know what you are doing?" I can trust you all I want, but if you don't have a clue what you are doing, what good is it? So your marketing message, must prove that you have experience.

3. *Education.* The third point demonstrates that you are trained, that you have specialized knowledge. It has to do with being an educational source as well as certification. We will cover all of these points in detail.

4. *Systems.* This point has to do with both the technical systems of your business as well as your customer service system. In other words, how will you service that client different from anyone else? If you are providing a technical, repair, or maintenance service, what is different about the service call compared to other companies?

5. *Guarantee.* The final point is to remove the risk of moving forward from the customer. The way you structure your guarantee has great impact on your message. More on this in just a moment.

Two Versions of the Message

There are two primary ways you will use this message:

1. Introduction version – Short, memorized

2. Presentation version – Longer, applied to the situation

The *introduction* version is used in any case in which you are in a position of "introducing" your company to a prospect (like the example of the CPA example earlier). If someone comes across a brochure about your company, it should deliver these five points. In the case of using it verbally (in the grocery store for example), you can cover all five points very effectively in about 60-90 seconds. Some people call this the "Elevator Pitch."

Now instead of using language that focuses on "how you do your work" like everyone else does, you are "refocusing" that prospect on the five things that set you apart. Using the five points, you will be able to convey a meaningful message in a short amount of time that will set you apart and will attract the right kind of prospects.

The longer, *presentation* version is used once you have generated prospects and you have the opportunity to give them a presentation. This may be over the phone or in person. The benefit of doing a presentation is that you can discover their needs and customize your five point message to fit their needs, concerns, and desires. (You will see this again in Phenomenal Sales Systems).

I call the Five Point "Experiential" Marketing Message a UEP™ (Unique Experience Proposition™). You may have heard of a USP (Unique Selling Proposition) in the past. Because Experiential Marketing is so important, I have changed that to a UEP.

How to Use the Five Points

Marketing Point #1: Reputation

Using Starbucks as our example, they have gained a reputation of being the coffee experts. They did this in two ways. One, they raise some real concerns about how average, everyday, commodity coffee is made. The worst stories tell how imported coffees use dirt as filler! They share how commodity coffees use an inferior bean called the Robusta bean. Starbucks use only 100 percent Arabica beans. Other coffee companies use conveyer belt roasting processes, and of course they have their own special, patented roasting system. Commodity coffee companies use harsh chemicals in the processing and have to use defoamer to smooth it out. Yuck!

Even though this focuses on the product, the reaction is purely emotional, and questions the integrity of other coffees. The emotional reaction is "yuck!" Once coffee is ground up, how do you know what's in there? Starbucks then begins the process of educating you about their processes that produce the *perfect cup.*

Marketing your reputation is done by using what others say about you rather than what you say about yourself! My friend Joseph Michelli, author of *The Starbucks Experience,* says "A brand is nothing more than what people say about you when you are not around." The relationships you have with your clients, people with influence in your industry and community will build your reputation and confirm that you can be trusted.

Testimonials are powerful ways to demonstrate trust, because what your clients and other important people say about you is more believable than what you say about yourself. Celebrity endorsements are also another great means if you can acquire it. If you have a local celebrity who recommends you, see if you can use that person's name in your marketing. For example, one of my companies was featured on a television show by a local celebrity. Our phone rang constantly, and we soon learned that he had a radio program where he would give live endorsements in the ads. We generated millions of dollars in sales over the years from that one source.

High profile projects or clients also help you develop your reputation (which translates into trust). Your involvement in community service speaks volumes. Awards and certifications are also great tools that build your reputation. Be sure to use all of these things in your marketing media.

What others say about you taps into a powerful human law called social proof. I was on the west side of Kauai, Hawaii, one day and the water was extremely rough. I noticed that other people were waiting to see if anyone drowned before they ventured in! This is social proof. Social proof says if others are doing it, it must be okay.

Be sure to communicate how each and every one of these marketing points benefit the client. This one is obvious. The benefit is that since you can trust our company, regardless of what happens, I know I am not going to be taken advantage of.

Introduction example of reputation: "Our company enjoys a reputation that is second to none. Some of the area's most seasoned <experts in your area> refer our services/products exclusively."

Marketing Point #2: Experience

Communicating your experience may be the number of years in business. "Since 1902" has an impact. "Over 20 years" is also a powerful statement. If the job requires a certain method of expertise or a certain procedure, you want to communicate your experience in those areas. One of the ways our service company made tremendous progress with our positioning was by offering to tackle troubleshooting jobs that no one else wanted to touch. Anything that was weird or far out, I wanted to get a peek at it. This in turn gave us unmatched experience. We were going after things that others were running from. In just a few years, I saw more situations that I was able to learn from than my competitors will likely see in a lifetime.

Introduction example of experience: "Our company has been in business for ____ years, and is experienced in all types of <whatever you do>. We will be familiar with your situation regardless of what it is unless…."

If you haven't been in business for very long, focus on the areas of experience you have. You can also lean heavier on the next point.

Marketing Point #3: Education (or Training)

If you are certified by your industry, you should educate your prospects and clients what certification means to them. Certification can be a powerful marketing tool, but only if you share what it means to you. Talk about any specialized training or knowledge you or your staff has that benefits them. And be sure to share that part of your mission is to educate them on how to navigate your industry. This sets you apart as a consultant.

Introduction example of education: "Our company is certified by the <Your Certification Group>. We are heavily involved in our industry to stay on the cutting edge of information. We bring this education directly to you so you can be sure you have the very best available."

Marketing Point #4: Systems

This is how you will deliver your unique experience. Your customer service system will set you apart more than anything else. And the best part is that it doesn't cost much more (if anything) to provide a higher level of customer service. The key is to not just provide it, but to talk about how it is different and use it in your marketing message.

Usually, customer frustrations have to do with service, not necessarily the product. By tapping into the emotional distress of the typical customer, you can win many new clients. What are they suffering from? Identify the areas where your competitors are failing to serve and promise to fill that gap. Be sure to explain exactly what you are going to do that is different.

Introduction example of systems: "Our mission is to provide you with the most phenomenal service experience ever. We will treat you with the utmost respect and courtesy and deliver your service/product on time."

In the longer version, you want to outline the steps you take that others don't.

Marketing Point #5: Guarantee

Many small business owners are afraid to offer a guarantee on their product or service in their marketing message, but when I ask them what happens if their client isn't satisfied, they quickly point out how they make it right including a refund if appropriate.

If you want to attract high-end clients, you must understand that they *expect* you to back up what you do. If there is any question about that, they will not move forward in using you. Using it in your marketing message confirms that you are the right company for them. If you are attracting price-shoppers or people who just want to get something for free from you, you are attracting the wrong crowd. And that is not because you are offering a guarantee, it's due to poor positioning.

Of course you are always going to have people who take advantage of your guarantee, so you factor that into your cost of doing business. If you can get more clients at higher prices because you offer a guarantee, you can actually make more money. Don't get emotional about this. Just work with the law of averages.

Of course there are many things that you can't offer a money back guarantee on. If you're a home builder, you can't give a refund on a house, but you can build a reputation that you follow up after the sale. My wife and I actually had this experience. We had a wonderful builder who addressed every need that came up long after the home was built and signed off on. That builder knows something that all business owners need to understand—how you handle your guarantee affects your reputation. So, you might imagine the five points being in a circle. Your guarantee is connected to your reputation.

Introduction example of guarantee: "Our company offers a 100 percent money back guarantee. If you are not completely thrilled with the service/product experience you receive from our company, we will rush back to your location at no charge and no obligation to correct the situation. If you are still unimpressed, you owe us nothing, and we will issue a 100 percent refund."

The Fastest Growth Tool on the Planet!

I would like to introduce you to a concept that is extremely valuable in marketing your company. It is a phenomenal tool to demonstrate your unique experience, and it's a fast growth tool because it makes it easy for a maximum number of people to "sample" your service.

It's called "The Free Trial Offer." This concept gives your prime target market the opportunity to experience your product or service before purchasing it. In the best case, it is an actual sample of the product or service. For example, Chick-fil-A began to offer a free trial in the malls. Now everyone does it. If you own a residential cleaning business, you would clean a room for free. If you have a golf club, offer a free round of golf to attract new prospects.

Did you know that Lexus has a free trial offer? When you go to the Lexus dealership and express interest in a car, they encourage you to take it home for the weekend. If you say, "I'm not sure I can get it back in time," they say "Don't worry! Bring it back when you can." You may say, "We'll I've got to go out of town this week." "Don't worry, we'll fill it up with gas. Take the car on the trip with you," they say.

What's happening here? They want you to take that car home with you because once you "experience" how it drives, you are going to want to keep it! And when you see how it looks in your driveway, now you really fall in love with it. But the kicker is when your neighbors come over and begin to ooh and ahh over it—there is no way that car is going back! Especially if you're a male! You know how that male ego is!

Zig Ziglar called that the "puppy dog" close. You know how it is when you bring a cute little puppy home. You fall in love with it and that little dude ain't going nowhere!

You might offer a free consultation, a free report, a free CD, video, webinars, or a free newsletter that offers tips and solutions to your prime target market's biggest frustrations and insights into helping them fulfill their biggest desires.

Make your free trial offer as impactful as possible. You want it to be informative, emotional, and you want it to get them to buy without pressure. This is a wonderful way for them to experience your product or service in action.

Instead of trying to take someone from suspect (someone who may or may not be a good prospect) straight to paying customer, the free trial offer takes them from suspect to prospect and allows you to do a very important thing—collect their contact information! Now you're in control of the follow up, not them. Plus, they have "raised their hand" for more information so to speak. They are telling you, "Hey, I'm a prospect! I'm interested!" All too often, prospects are skeptical and they want to "check you out." The free trial is the perfect way for them to get to know, like, and trust you.

What if people take advantage of your free trial? What if you have a free trial offer and it costs you money to provide the free product or service, or if there is a cost in delivering or installing the product? If you are a restaurant, a free meal costs money. How do you know if they will come back? You don't. But your goal is to create so many more clients as a result of your free trial that even if you get a few "freebies" who take advantage, you are still making more money.

Special note: Don't confuse the concept of the free trial with a discount! This is a completely different concept. A discount is "conditional" and causes prospects to respond to get a "deal." They still have to buy. The concept of a free trial offer is different because it allows them to experience you without risk.

How to Generate an Unlimited Supply of the Highest Paying Clients (without expensive advertising)

Everyone agrees that "word of mouth" is the best advertising. Everyone knows the power in one person telling another about a service or a product. The problem is that casual referrals usually don't create a phenomenally successful business. To generate a massive number of referrals, you need a phenomenal referral marketing *system*.

The second biggest marketing mistake small business owners make is what I call "chasing suspects." We've all been there. We chase people we think might be good prospects for us, trying to convince them of that, and we spend a massive amount of time and energy chasing them and nothing ever comes from it. Of course the "the fortune *is* in the follow up," but *who* you follow up with is very important. We should have a follow up system for those who are truly prospects. A suspect is someone who fits the demographic. A prospect is someone who has actually *asked* for more information.

The Secret to Record Sales and Profits

My experience of coaching thousands of small business owners around the world tells me that most small business owners are missing out on a very big secret. This is how I have built my companies and how small businesses worldwide are having record sales and profits. The secret is this: *Instead of chasing suspects and spending so much time following up with individual prospects, invest your time building relationships with powerful referral sources.*

What I mean by a referral *source* is a company or professional that has a relationship with an unlimited supply of your perfect niche client. For example, if you are a CPA and you get referrals from attorneys, then your referral source would be law firms. Invest your time building relationships with attorneys who can refer an unlimited supply of your perfect niche client.

Here are a few examples: Currently, I'm the exclusive small business coaching arm for the Ziglar Corporation. They are a referral source for me. There are many small business owners (my niche) on their list. Also, I'm a referral source for Ziglar. Who needs Zig Ziglar products? Everyone! All of my clients need their products.

Not too long after I began teaching my systems to small business owners, I approached a large supplier that had thousands of small business owner customers across the nation. We put together a joint venture, and I travelled to their stores all over the country and they made sure the small business owners were there to learn from me.

The first company I started is a cleaning business that cares for Oriental rugs, stone floors, and fine carpets. It was built by building relationships with flooring retailers, interior designers, and real estate agents. They refer their clients to us exclusively.

My first book was an Amazon.com number one best seller because I coordinated a launch with a dozen "affiliates" that promoted my book to their list.

My Definition of Referral Marketing: "The process of building a *network* of *sources* that will *refer* multiple clients to your business."

Top Ten Reasons Referral Marketing is so Effective

1. *Your Network is Unlimited.* As you begin to build relationships with powerful referral sources and you get your clients to refer you, the network continues to grow with no end in sight.

2. *Higher Quality Clients.* Since Mercedes' clients seek out a referral, you get higher quality clients just from being "referral based." Referred clients usually don't even ask about the price. They are more concerned about quality than price.

3. *Pre-Qualified Clients.* By educating your referral sources, your prospective clients will be pre-qualified; therefore they will already know more about you (and that you charge more than the commodity or service level company).

4. *People Trust Referrals.* Wouldn't you agree that referrals already have a level of trust for you? Sure they do. They trust you because the person they trust knows you.

5. *Reduces Competition.* With referral marketing, you are no longer fighting for the best ad placement or getting copied. Relationships are hard to duplicate.

6. *Low Cost.* With the right referral marketing system, you won't spend money on expensive advertising. The cost is very low for referral marketing. Even with a Referral Reward Program (which I highly recommend), the cost is still extremely low compared to most advertising.

7. *High Returns.* The returns can potentially be huge. In many industries a 4 to 1 return on investment on advertising dollars would be outstanding. In other words, if you invested $1,000 in advertising, you would get an average of $4,000 in return. With referral marketing, if you pay a 10 percent referral reward and

everyone cashed in on it, you would have a 10-to-1 return. In my reward program, I get a 20-to-1 return as less than half of the certificates are ever redeemed.

8. *Returns Guaranteed.* With a referral reward, you don't pay it until *after* the product or service is paid for. With traditional advertising, you put your money on the line and hope for a return.

9. *Small-Time Investment.* The biggest objection I get to referral marketing is "time." See #10 to overcome that challenge.

10. *Expo-nen-tial Multiplication!* Would you be interested in how investing just a few minutes a day doing something really fun would give you a return of over $10,000 in new business each and every month after six months? Of course you would. Even though I can't guarantee it, I have seen it happen many times.

Here's what I discovered with referral marketing (see chart).

Exponential Multiplication Chart

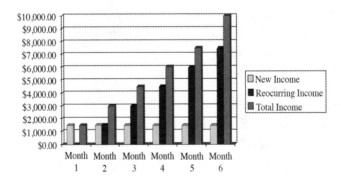

If you invested just thirty minutes per day calling on powerful referral sources (companies that are in a position to refer you on a regular basis), do you think it's possible to generate just $1,500 in new referrals in a one-month period? See the first column on the chart. Not too difficult for most small businesses.

What I discovered about referral marketing is that once you win the confidence of a referral source, they will continue the habit of referring you (the light column), unless you give them a reason not to. You will then continue to develop new referral sources each month to the tune of $1,500 each month.

All told, at the end of six months, you would be at over $10,000 per month in *new* referred business! The total monthly income in new business is demonstrated by the second darker column.

This is how I built my first company from the trunk of my car to a multimillion dollar enterprise. I still use this method today. This is how I built a phenomenal training business and the reason you are holding this book in your hand right now. And it's the same method I have taught countless small business owners around the world. They are having record sales and profits because of it. Finally, it will work for you too if you understand it and apply it.

All of Business is About Relationships

Would you agree that all of business and all of life is about relationships? You bet. So the idea here is to build relationships with potential referral sources. By adding value to them, they will add value to you.

Have you ever heard "It's not *what* you know it's *who* you know"? Over the past 28 years in business, I have learned that *all* of business is about relationships. But, it's not just *who* you know, but *what* you *know* about who you know.

And it's not about who *you* know—but who knows *you* and *what* they know about you. That's called *positioning*. My good friend Bob Burg, bestselling author of *The Go-Giver,* says that people do business with those they know, like, and trust.

Are You Building Phenomenal Relationships?

Are you actively building phenomenal relationships? Or are you just relying on casual word of mouth or advertising to get customers? How much time do you invest in business relationships? Or are you kind of stuck "in" your business?

In today's digital world, we are more connected, but more isolated than ever before. I personally love social networking and actively network on Facebook, but I also make time to connect face to face, because nothing can replace that.

American legend Zig Ziglar said, "You can have everything in life you want, if you just help enough other people get what they want."

Jesus said, "Give and it will be given back to you, pressed down, shaken together and running over." It may not come from the same person, but my experience has shown me that if you give people what they want, they will be more apt to give you want you want.

Jim Cathcart, best-selling author of *Relationship Selling,* says that "relationship selling is becoming an asset to others *before* they become an asset to you." So when you want to build a relationship with someone who can benefit your business, find out what they like, what they want, and what they need—and simply be the one to give it to them.

Best-selling author Jeffrey Gitomer says, "All things being equal, people would rather do business with a friend. All things being not so equal, people would still rather do business with a friend."

You see, you can have higher prices and a longer wait, but your referral sources will still support you because you are a trusted friend and advisor. While others are begging at the front door, trying to get by the gatekeeper, you are being graciously invited in through the back door.

If people don't know about you, they obviously can't use you or refer you. If they don't like you, they don't use you or refer you unless they absolutely have to. And if they don't trust you, they won't use you or refer you.

Finally, building relationships requires leadership on your part. My good friend John C. Maxwell (the world's number one leadership expert) says that leadership is influence. Nothing more, nothing less. We all have influence in other people's lives. How do you get influence? By adding value to others. John says, "If you don't add value to others, you de-value them." Add value to them, and they will add value to you.

Remember, *all* of business is about *relationships.* You can know everything there is to know about the technical part of your business—and be *broke!* Not to say that being technically savvy isn't important. It is. But you can be the most "technical" person in the world, but be broke in business.

The Value of Becoming a Phenomenal Networker

To build a phenomenal referral marketing system, you need to understand networking and how to build rapport quickly.

First, dress well. Did you know that people make 11 important assumptions about you in the first 30 seconds of meeting you? Most of this happens before you even open your mouth! First impressions last, so you want to make it a good one!

My personal view is that this is an area where many small business owners and professionals are failing. We have become so casual in our culture that we aren't even aware of the impact of dressing professionally. You'll learn in the leadership chapter that leadership is influence. You influence others in how you dress and groom yourself. Positively or negatively.

My goal is to always be dressed sharp without over-doing it. If you are going to build powerful business relationships, you need to look like a businessperson. Wear a sport coat and a tie if you are a man. Wear a dress or nice pantsuit if you are a woman.

Make sure your clothing is professionally pressed, your shoes are shined and your accessories are appropriate. Your hair should be well groomed, your fingernails clipped and clean; be clean shaven, and keep some breath mints with you at all times! No one likes spending time with someone whose breath could melt butter!

Always have business cards (or brochures) with you. Don't go *anywhere* without business cards! Keep a stack in your pocket, a stack in the car, and keep your extra supply wherever you keep your car keys! When you meet people, always get *their* cards. It is much more important for you to get their cards, because there is no guarantee that they will call you, so be sure to follow up with them.

Be gracious. When you are in a networking environment, you are not there for you! You're not there to eat and take advantage of the food and drink. You are there to build relationships, so prefer others before yourself. Be polite and kind. Be positive and likeable.

Avoid getting into negative conversations. Sometimes you will run into people at networking groups who want to talk about the weather or complain about the food, or whatever. Keeping in mind that you are not there for you, avoid these conversations. They are not productive and they bring everybody down.

Don't stand in the corner all alone. Instead, identify those who could be good referral sources for you and strike up a conversation. When you begin speaking with them, instead of being anxious to share what *you* do, show interest in what *they* do. Find out as much as you can about them and their business. This will come in handy when you get to talk about your business. People love nothing more than to talk about themselves and their business. In fact, a great exercise is to practice asking as many questions as possible without saying anything about yourself until they ask. Once they ask, that means they will listen closer to what you have to say.

Listen emphatically. Instead of half way listening (called "selective" listening), listen closely to what the other person is saying. Use nods and positive affirmations to let them know you are interested in what they are saying.

Even if you aren't, you should be—at least from the standpoint of how you will build a professional relationship with this person. Try to discover ways you can help them with their business and add value to them.

Remember why you are there! You are there to build your business. To build relationships, to find out how you can help others so they will in turn help you. You are not there for personal reasons. Keep your goals in mind and make the time investment worthwhile.

Follow Up

Immediately put their name and address into a database. Every card you gather, immediately put the information into a database. If you are strapped for time, hire a high school or college student to do data entry for you. Then follow up immediately by sending the new contact a "Nice to Meet You" letter or card and an info pack. You should develop an information pack that shows why prospects should use you over someone else.

Mail something to them every month. Depending on your business, you should be mailing or emailing your clients and prospects every month to develop repeat business, referrals, and secure your position as the obvious choice.

Put them on your calendar to call the following week or whenever you told them you would call. Remember, the "fortune is in the follow up." But also remember that your goal is to make so many contacts that you don't have to chase individual suspects to survive.

Download my free, step-by-step networking script that is proven to build rapport. Just scan the QR Code or click this link: http://www.howardpartridge.com/networking

The Secret Weapon!

Once you have identified past referral sources, you now have a profile of potential referral sources. You have a reward system in place. Now it's time to make a visit to their office or store. There is one secret strategy that will do more for your referral relationship program than anything else.

What is this powerful secret? Food. Yes, food. In particular, donuts, chocolates, pizza, lunch, candy, snacks, etc. Food is the international language that everyone understands! Food is the one thing that can gain the attention that you cannot get any other way. The reason is that feeding someone taps deep into the Law of Reciprocity, which says, "If you give me something, I give you something." With food it goes deeper. It penetrates our most primitive make up. If you feed me, I owe you the time of day. If you give me a treat, I owe you at least a couple minutes of time!

Remember the Five Point Marketing Message from earlier? What a great time to share it—while they are partaking of the delicious brownies or candy you just brought! If you walk in with sales materials, what's their posture? Busy! Too busy to talk. But if you walk in the door with a box of Krispy

Kreme donuts, they will listen to every word you have to say! It's amazing, and I have seen it work over and over again.

I first learned this from my wife, Denise. She's in radio sales, and I noticed that she would take her clients milk and cookies in the afternoon, bring them lunch. She even had a company that made custom chocolate bars and she had the client's logo branded on the chocolate bar.

Just about every night she's wrapping gifts for clients and people in her network. All of the closets in our house are jammed with gifts that don't belong to anyone yet. She buys things as she sees them, then when there's a need, the wrapping begins! I finally "got it" one hot summer morning when she was walking out the door to go to work with a laundry basket full of things for the pool—squirt guns, goggles, and flip flops. "Where ya goin' with that stuff?" I asked. "Oh, a lot of my clients have kids, so I'm bringing them stuff for the pool." *Hmmm...,* I thought to myself.

I decided to try it out.

There was a large potential referral source that I had called on 11 times (yes, *eleven* times). I had nice brochures and a nice introduction, but I didn't have the secret weapon. Every time I went into this place, I got the same response—a stiff arm came up along with, "We're real happy with the people we're using right now. Thanks for coming by." But this time I went to the grocery store and bought a little box of chocolates for $2.99.

I walked in and a lady down the hall noticed me come in. I introduced myself and she responded with the same stiff arm answer. She obviously didn't see the chocolates, so I said, "But I brought chocolates" with a little smile on my face. You should have seen her body language change! It went from the Nazi stiff arm to standing in front of me holding the box of chocolates almost close to her heart. I could almost hear her thinking, *Who is this nice man bringing me chocolates!* Within seven days we began getting referrals from that company. And they became a consistent referral source for us from that point on.

One of my early members increased his business $30,000 per month by making Friday "Donut Day." He and his wife loaded up the truck with branded boxes of donuts every week and set out to see as many referral sources and accounts as they could. I ran into him at a conference recently, and he told me it continued to work so well that he now has other people delivering donuts on a regular basis. That is the case with us as well.

A final food story that is instructive is about an auto repair shop called Freedom Automotive. My service company has a nice clean fleet of vehicles parked outside. Freedom Automotive obviously noticed the fleet, and one morning a box of donuts and a little card from Freedom Automotive showed up at our office. The next week, another box of donuts. After about the fourth or fifth week, I saw my operations director walking down the hall with a fistful of donuts and Freedom's card. He said, "We should at least give them a try." (I mean after all, they might stop sending us donuts if we don't, right?)

So we called Freedom, and they came to the office and gave us a presentation. They charged more than the shop we currently used. "Yeah, but the shop we use doesn't even say thank you. They don't care about us," we argued to ourselves. In Freedom's presentation, they showed us how following their maintenance plan would actually save us money. Who do you think we use? Freedom Automotive. This took place about 20 years ago, and we still use them today. I know what you're wondering, *Do they still have donuts delivered?* Yes, they still have donuts delivered.

Find out what your major accounts and your referral sources like and take it to them. If they like Dove bars, take Dove bars to them. If they like Starbucks chocolate-covered Espresso beans, bring those along with you when you visit.

We have all of our existing and potential referral sources on a route. Every month we deliver cookies, pies, cakes, or whatever. We have a number of other "food strategies" too. For example, we cook breakfast for referral sources, hold referral appreciation lunches, and more.

What if your referral sources aren't local? You can ship stuff. There are a variety of gourmet food baskets you can order online. Recently a man who owns a franchise called Candy Bouquet International became a client of ours—they make custom candy bouquets. I use a program called Send Out Cards (the greatest marketing tool of all time, which I will talk about later). With Send Out Cards, you can send along cookies, brownies, and many other gourmet food items.

Who Likes Money?

Have you noticed that most people like money? Zig used to say, "Money isn't the most *important* thing in life, but it *is reasonably* close to oxygen!" To maximize your referrals, you should definitely offer a financial reward. You will get more referrals and your advertising dollars will go down. Sure you can get referrals without a reward, but you will get much more if you offer a reward. Plus, offering a referral reward gives you something to talk about. If you don't offer a reward of some kind, it makes it harder to ask for referrals without appearing selfish. Remember, everyone listens to the same radio station: WIIFM (What's In It For Me).

A good referral reward program offers anyone who refers a new client to you a reward. You offer cash or products and services. Example: Suzy refers Bob who is a new client. Bob spends $500 with you and your referral reward is 10 percent. You mail a Referral Reward Certificate to Suzy for $50. She can then redeem that certificate for services or she can cash it in. It's best to give them a choice. It can be a flat fee instead of a percentage of sale if you like, but make it significant.

Now, Suzy receives this wonderful Referral Reward Certificate and she can decide whether she wants to redeem it, throw it away, or give it to someone else. Here's where it gets interesting. The certificate is just like cash and can be given to a favorite charity, a friend, or whatever the person wants to do with it. Suzy doesn't want to take money from you and doesn't need your service or product right now, but she has another friend who does!

Suzy refers Cathy. Cathy calls you up or walks into your store and says, "Can I use this certificate?" "You bet!" you say. Cathy spends $500 with you and you take $50 off (the value of the certificate). Now her bill is $450. She is a new client referred by Suzy and Suzy will now get *another* certificate for $45 for referring Cathy. Does Suzy have more friends?

You bet she does!

At this point, you are probably thinking, *Boy, that sounds like a lot of money to give away.* Let me ask you this question: Do you know what it cost you to gain a new client? For example, if you invest $1,000 in advertising, would you be happy with a $4,000 initial return? If so, that just cost you *25 percent* to gain that new client.

"But, Howard, I already get referrals," you might say. My experience of implementing this with business owners around the world is that you'll get more referrals. And by the way, don't people deserve a reward for going out of their way to support your business?

Our experience in most small businesses is that less than 50 percent of the certificates ever get cashed in for one reason or another. Also, put an expiration date on the certificate. We use a one year expiration.

How much should you offer? Determine what your new client acquisition cost is and go from there. We offer 10 percent in my service company. Anyone who refers a new client gets a referral certificate for 10 percent of the first job. After that, they are a repeat client. Less than half of the certificates are ever redeemed, so I am only spending 5 percent to gain a new client (that's a 20-to-1 return by the way). What's more impressive is that the referral rewards we actually pay out are less than 1 percent of our total revenue.

My coaching company uses what is called an "affiliate program," which is much like a referral program. The difference is that when you have a company that is well known in a certain community or industry, your prospects come to know about you through a variety of channels. Companies that do a lot of direct advertising using multiple channels don't always know exactly what ad triggered the sale (unless they have trackable phone numbers, promo numbers, or links if it is online). So an affiliate program (especially online) is beneficial. This way, an affiliate (referral source) can have a special code and put someone on our list using a special link. When their referral buys a product or attends a workshop, the affiliate gets 50 percent. When that person joins our coaching program, they get a flat $300.

So you can offer a percentage or a flat fee, but you must make sure it is attractive enough for people to take the extra step to refer you. Is everyone motivated by money? No. Can everyone accept a reward? No. Some industries have rules against referral rewards or commissions. Therefore, we put on our certificate: "If you have a conflict of interest or cannot accept this reward, please pass on to your client or someone else."

Simply put, here's how our referral reward program works. We promote it on everything we print, everywhere we go, anything we do by saying, "Get Free CASH or FREE <Your Service or Product Goes Here> with Our Referral Reward Program!"™* Every time a new customer buys from us, we have a system of recording how they were referred (online and offline). They are tagged as being referred by that person. Then we have a process of sending referral certificates or affiliate funds to that person. It's as simple as that. *If you are not one of our coaching clients yet, please change this significantly to protect the interest of our members. Thank you for your integrity.

I'm sure you have more questions about a referral reward program, but my challenge is that I don't have enough space and time in this book to teach you the "ins and outs" of a proper referral program. Also, getting the details right will be the difference of it working or not, so scan the following QR code to see how you can get our training program on how to create your own referral reward program for your business.

One final note: If you offer a referral reward, be sure to honor it and pay it promptly! The worst thing you can do is promote a referral reward and fail to pay it.

To get a Free Report on how my Referral Reward Program works, scan the QR Code or click this link: www.howardpartridge.com/referralreward

Advanced Referral Marketing Strategies

Once you build a solid relationship with referral sources and you are giving them the top three things they cherish (support, food, and money!), you can take it to the next level with these advanced strategies:

Cook Breakfast or Lunch: We have a system in place where we go to a client's site and cook bacon and eggs, fajitas, etc. for our referral sources. One of my clients built a really cool trailer with a grill on it. They do fajitas and barbeque for their referral sources.

The Free Lunch Program: Hold a Referral Appreciation Luncheon at a top restaurant. Invite past, existing, and potential referral sources to thank them for their support. We give out prizes, present a short talk, and even show video testimonials.

Group Marketing: The power of event marketing is that you are getting groups of referral sources together, which saves you a ton of time and also positions you as the expert. Events create memorable experiences as well. It creates a sense of community. Set up a Q&A or an educational talk for your referral sources, hold educational events (even get them approved for continuing education credits) or webinars. This positions you as the expert.

Even if you bring in a speaker, you are the one who is making the experience possible.

Golf Tournaments and Charity Events: Get involved in events that your referral sources are involved in. Serve and support them and hopefully get the microphone!

Joint Mailers: Your referral sources send your phenomenal information to their clients to add value to them. This generates even more referrals as you are targeting a niche audience that has a relationship with the referral source.

As you can see, there are many referral marketing strategies you can use. And my experience is that referral marketing is the key to creating record sales and profits serving the niche clients you want to serve.

How to Double Your Business in the Next 12 Months (without adding a single customer!)

Does your business rely on repeat business? Is your primary referral source your past or existing customers? If so, you are probably committing the biggest marketing mistake of all (other than doing nothing).

The biggest marketing mistake of all is not marketing to your past customers. Statistics reveal that it costs 500 percent more to gain a new client than to keep an existing one. Did you also know that without consistent marketing, many of your clients would forget about you and eventually end up using someone else? It's a hard fact to swallow, but it's true.

A few years ago I participated in a home show with some service industry associates. After surveying a good portion of the attending homeowners, we discovered that they could not remember the name of the service company they had recently used—even though they were thrilled with the work—even when the service had been just two weeks prior! The company did a good job, but will never be in that home again unless they correct this HUGE mistake.

A multi-industry study by the Wharton School of Business at the University of Pennsylvania revealed that companies who increased their customer retention rate by a mere 5 to 11 percentage points actually increased their profits by an astounding 25 to 75 percent, depending on the industry!

It is my belief (and experience) that you can double your business in the next 12 months without actually adding a single customer. In 1999 I proved the theory in my service company by simply increasing my mailing frequency from quarterly to monthly. Eight additional months of mailing to past clients over a one year period cost about $16,000 in printing and postage, but the return was over $200,000 in trackable additional business!

Are you tracking your repeat business? Are you tracking your referrals? Are you tracking the returns on your advertising dollars? If you aren't, I can guarantee you are leaving money on the table. We'll talk about that in Phenomenal Administration Systems.

A Sad Story

My wife and I frequented one of the finest restaurants in the Houston area. I worked there when I started my first business. We were engaged there and celebrated many anniversaries there. The owners of the restaurant died and two sisters who worked there took over the restaurant. They weren't very good marketers and business became very slow. Every time we saw them they complained about how bad business was. My wife and I made suggestions, but they didn't seem very interested.

We knew they weren't doing many of the basic things they should be doing to get business. One night as we were talking with one of the ladies, she was labeling post cards. Real nice post cards. I remembered them from when I worked there. Gesturing toward the post card, I asked, "How well do those post cards pull?"

"Oh, phenomenal!" she said. "Every time we send them out we get tons of business. People come in and buy dinner and wine and sometimes they even bring friends with them." This was the first positive thing I had heard her say in three years! Then I asked,

"How often do you send them out?"

"About once a year," she replied.

I was shocked! Why do you think she didn't send them out more often? "Because it costs so much," she said. After being one of the top restaurants in Houston, Texas, for over 25 years, that restaurant closed its doors. Out of business. Why? Bad food? No. Poor service? No. Just a lack of marketing knowledge. Sad.

Most small business owners don't understand the value of marketing to past clients. All they see is the cost. Then they want to go cheap and just mail to them or reach them by social media. Big mistake! A printed newsletter, post card, or greeting card has much more staying power than an email that can easily be overlooked or deleted. Just yesterday I had one of my coaching clients tell me that sometimes my emails I send to her don't get read, but when I send a newsletter, she places it on the corner of her desk until it gets read!

To further irritate the problem, most small business owners don't know how to track their repeat business. Tracking repeat business is completely different from tracking returns on paid advertising. With paid advertising, you invest a dollar and you track how many dollars you got back in new business. Many times when you market to your past clients, they may not respond to the offer, but they do remember you when they need you. Let me give you an example.

I was talking to a coaching client about this and he said, "My client-based marketing isn't working." "Okay, tell me what you are doing," I probed. He told me that he was sending post cards with an offer, but no one was calling.

"No one?" I asked.

"Nobody" he confirmed.

"So, you're telling me that you didn't have *one single repeat client* over the past three months?"

"Well of course I have," he said.

"Then why would you say your client mailers aren't working?"

I went on to explain that the way you measure the effectiveness of your client-based marketing system is by tracking the *total* repeat customer dollars compared to the same period last year. Your goal is for that number to keep growing. It's the difference between a savings account with interest and day-trading stocks. A savings account grows over time and collects interest. Your total balance continues to grow. Direct advertising is more like day trading. You make an investment and get an immediate return on it.

Client-based marketing is more like a drip rather than a one-shot deal. Sure you can have strong offers, but be careful to protect the permission you have so you can build a long-term relationship for long-term results as well.

When marketing to your client base (mailing, calling, emailing), another hidden question to consider is, "How much are you *losing* by not staying in touch?" This is a hidden cost factor that is often overlooked.

Before even asking what the returns will be, consider what you are losing. You are losing valuable clients every day by not at least staying in touch. But for the sake of argument, let's say that you have 1,000 clients and it costs you $750 per month to mail to them. That would be $9,000 per year. If you could add $80,000 in revenue, don't you think it would be worth the investment? Even if it only increased your business by $36,000, it would be worth it. Plus, repeat clients are easier to service, they already know your prices, and you don't have to "sell" them. My experience has been that the long-term results will be more significant than that.

Five Steps to Double Your Business (without adding one customer)

1. *Get a higher price.* One of the reasons to constantly be in front of your past and existing clients (other than the fact that your competitor is marketing to them), is to reinforce your brand message that positions you at a higher value. Translation: higher price. Constantly remind them of the reasons to always use you and build the unique experience around your company.

2. *TOMA (Top Of Mind Awareness).* Just because you did a great job doesn't mean your customers will remember you. I had $6,000 worth of plumbing done in my commercial building. I completely forgot about the plumber who had serviced my home on occasion. Why? Because he doesn't have a system to stay in touch. Do you? How many of your customers are gone because of it?

3. *Sell more products and services.* You probably have a variety of products and services in addition to your main product or service. Marketing to your past clients can dramatically increase your income and profit margin!

4. *Increase frequency of use.* Getting your clients to purchase more often is another powerful thing that can add lots of dollars to your business.

5. *Referrals!* If your clients have trouble remembering your name, much less all the wonderful things that set you apart, what are the chances they are going to be good referral sources? No chances! A strong client-based marketing program can dramatically increase your referrals, especially if you have a Referral Reward Program.

The Most Phenomenal Marketing Tool of All Time

Many of the country's top business trainers and marketers have recognized me as being a phenomenal marketer, so when I call something the most phenomenal marketing tool of *all time,* that's a BIG statement! This is a tool that I have been using for over five years at this writing. It's a tool that *any* small business owner or professional can use. And it's also a way that anyone can make money.

Now before I reveal what this amazing tool is, let's remind ourselves that all of business is about relationships and building your network of relationships is the most important business skill you can have. Building those relationships and staying in touch with your past clients are *the two most important marketing activities* you can be implementing.

Having said that, would you agree that one of the most meaningful tools you could use would be a heartfelt, personalized greeting card? This is probably one of the most valuable ways you can communicate to someone. Much better than email and way better than a promotional advertising piece.

But here's the problem...

To consistently write a personal greeting card to everyone in your network and on your client base list is nearly impossible. But what if there was a way to send meaningful greeting cards that not only touch the heart, but also position you as the consultant and remind your contacts to support you?

What if the business cards that you collected at a networking group weren't rotting away in a desk drawer, but were actually put into a system that was creating powerful relationships that can add great value to your life and career?

You can solve those problems with the most phenomenal marketing tool of all time! What is that tool? It's called Send Out Cards, a greeting card company where you can choose from thousands of greeting cards and they will mail the card for you in a white envelope that looks handwritten.

Why do I call this the most phenomenal marketing tool of *all* time? Here's why. Not only can you just jump on the Website and send a card (through the U.S. postal system—it is *not* an ecard). And not only does it look personal and handwritten like an invitation, with a real stamp (incidentally, the reason that is important is people *always* open personal greeting cards or invitations).

You can even use your own handwriting and signature! You fill out a little form and send it to Send Out Cards, and they load your handwriting and signatures (you may have several, perhaps one from you and your spouse or business partner). Now if your handwriting is as bad as mine, you might want to skip that option, but it gets better.

You can even create your own card quickly and easily and insert any picture that is on your computer. And remember, Send Out Cards sends that card through the mail in an envelope for as low as 93 cents plus postage at the time of this writing. Send a card without a picture for as low as 62 cents plus postage.

Here are a few examples of how powerful this can be. Let's say you have a meeting with someone or you meet someone at a networking group. You take a picture with that person. Simply upload that picture and send him or her a card. Easy as that. I have a standard "Nice To Meet You" Card Template in Send Out Cards.

Where can you get a full color, custom piece in an envelope that you can have designed and mailed today for less than a dollar—in a quantity of one—in five minutes?

When you collect business cards at a networking group, just have an assistant, a high school or college student (or even one of your children) enter the business card into the program and launch your "Nice To Meet You" card template that you've already designed.

Now, here's the interesting part, where it gets even better…

Not only can you create a card with any picture on your computer, you can send that same card to a whole group of people in your database. Each card is personalized to each person! How cool is that? Here are a few examples. Let's say you have a small database of clients. Simply create a card, and send it to the entire list. Your holiday and seasonal cards just became a breeze! Let's say you belong to a networking group that has 35 members. You take a picture at the meeting and send it out to the entire group.

It gets even better....

Phenomenal Relationship Marketing means remembering birthdays and anniversaries. Send Out Cards has an automatic reminder system for that.

Gets even better...

Along with the card, you can send chocolates, brownies, cookies, gift cards (like American Express, Starbucks, Home Depot), books, CDs, and many other gifts.

Gets even better!

You can create automatic multi-card campaigns. Earlier in the book I shared the importance of educating clients and staying in touch with them. A very important process is to "teach" new customers how to be great clients and how to refer you properly. So you have a series of cards that starts with a thank you card. Next is a card that focuses on the referral program. Next a card that features one of your services, and so on.

Once you activate the multi-card campaign for a contact, Send Out Cards will automatically remember to send the card on a certain interval. If you think about it long enough you could activate a year-long "Why I Like You" Card campaign! Reason #1... Reason #2...

To use Send Out Cards, you will need a Sponsor ID. Contact whoever gave you this book to get their sponsor ID.

The Phenomenal Potential Lifetime Value (PLV) of a Client

In his book *The Facts of Business Life*, my friend Bill McBean says a business owner's first responsibility is to protect its assets. Not just the assets on the balance sheet, but your database as well. My good friend and marketing master David Frey says, "The money is in the list!" Not just the number of people on the list, but the quality of the list. And the quality of the relationships you've developed with them.

Have you ever thought about the value of your list? Have you ever thought about the *potential lifetime value* (PLV) of a single client? This exercise will astound you and from this moment on you will have a greater appreciation for your clients. Far too often a customer's value is judged by a single transaction. They bought a low-priced product or did a minimum job. It's about the long-term value of that client and their referrals.

Many years ago when I was first starting out, I quoted a very low minimum charge over the phone, assuming it was a "minimum" job. Upon arriving, I realized I had totally underpriced myself for the project. Instead of making excuses, I smiled and went to work. After all, it wasn't her fault that I didn't have a good pricing system! Turns out the client was the facilities manager for the *largest* branch banking system in Texas at the time, which became my biggest account the next day. I made a *lot* of money from that bank for many years. Had I made excuses and judged her based on how much money she spent with me on that first project, I would have never gotten the big account.

Take a moment to jot down the average amount a single client invests with you each year. Now multiply that by 20 years. Example: Let's say a single client invests $2,000 per year with you. Twenty years x $2,000 = $40,000. Now, multiply that number by the number of referrals you could potentially get. Let's say it's just two per year. That's an additional $80,000 in potential lifetime value, giving you a total potential lifetime value of $120,000!

This is how you should look at the economic value of clients (while also remembering that they are human beings who should be treated well). Are you planning on being around for 20 years? I've been in business over 28 years at this writing. Protect your assets. The most valuable asset is your client list. When you sell your business, the predictable income is probably going to be the biggest factor. And by the way, if you teach your team to value customers at this level, will it make a difference in how they see them? You bet it will.

Phenomenal Direct Advertising

Direct Advertising is when you place an advertisement to reach your end user client. Phenomenal Direct Advertising is when you generate your perfect niche prospect. A Phenomenal Direct Advertising System duplicates results consistently.

Although direct advertising can bring you phenomenal results in some industries if it is done right, it is not a place to "wing it." Direct adverting usually isn't cheap, and I've seen too many business owners literally go broke paying for ads that never had a prayer of working!

1. *What results do you want?* Anytime you are using paid advertising, be sure to understand what return on investment (ROI) you are looking for. In other words, when you advertise for $1, how many do you need to get in return? Many times you won't know this until testing the ad, which is the reason I do mostly relationship marketing. Direct advertising can be costly. On the other hand, we have done paid advertising for my companies that have generated huge returns.

2. *Who is your advertising target audience?* The first thing to think about when advertising is who your audience is. At any given time, you may be placing advertising to reach:

- *A Suspect* (someone who fits the demographic of your perfect niche market).

- *A Prospect* (someone who has already expressed interest, but has not become a customer yet).

- *A Customer or Client* (someone who has purchased before). In this case you want to generate repeat business, sell additional products and services, or to compel the customer or client to move to a higher level membership, or something of that nature.

Each of these audiences require a different approach because your permission level is different, what they know about you is different, and what you want them to do is different. You may need to have a process of moving suspects to prospects before they become a customer. A customer is different from a client. An advocate or raving fan is someone who has moved beyond client status. You market to them differently.

3.   *What do you want them to do?* When you are placing an ad or presenting a message to an audience, think about what action you want them to take as a result of the message. Start with the end in mind. Do you want them to call you? Do you want them to opt-in for something? If you are speaking to a group, do you want them to come up to you afterward? Do you want them to fill out a form? Do you want them to buy something? If so, what? This is called your *call to action.* We'll talk about that in a moment.

4.   *What message do you want to deliver?* What message is going to get them to take the action you want them to take?

How to Create a Phenomenal Marketing Message

There are plenty of books and resources on writing copy, so I won't attempt to teach you everything you need to know. Plus, one book won't do the job. The good news is you don't have to be an expert copywriter to be successful in marketing your business, but understanding how to structure a message will help you in all areas of your marketing, whether it is addressing a group of referral sources or creating a brochure. But it is *vital* to the success of any direct advertising you do.

Three Vital Components of Creating Phenomenal Marketing Copy

1. A Phenomenal Headline

Your headline is the main heading in a print ad, or the first words spoken in an audio message. It has been said that the headline constitutes 80 percent of your ad's effectiveness. After all, if it doesn't even get noticed, what's it really worth?

Here are some tips to create a dynamic headline:

- The headline should draw your readers in. The headline should get their attention so they will be intrigued to read more. Some have called the headline "the ad for the ad."

- The headline should say as much as possible. In other words, the headline should give as much information about the following message as possible. Obviously you are limited, but keep crafting the headline until it says the precise thing that you want readers to know if that's *all* you could tell them. Long headlines, subheads, and text on top of the headline are all good ways to accomplish this.

- Mention benefits. Readers are interested in what you can do for *them*. What is the benefit to *them?* Write what the service *does,* rather than what it is. Put benefits in your headline.

- Get emotional. Use emotionally charged words rather than technical or feature-based words. See the following list of the thirteen most powerful words in advertising.

- Target to only your audience. The more you can pre-qualify your prospects in advertising, the fewer unqualified calls you will generate. Use copy that will appeal to your target market only.

- Don't use tired clichés. Don't use worn out, meaningless phrases. Clichés don't work, and they don't really mean anything significant.

Headline samples:

- Avoid Uneducated, Uninformed, and Sometimes Downright Unscrupulous Plumbers!

- Avoid Uneducated, Uninformed, and Sometimes Downright Unscrupulous Air Conditioning Companies!

- *Instead, get the Most Outstanding Service Experience Ever!*

- Avoid Uneducated, Uninformed, and Sometimes Downright Unscrupulous Landscaping Companies!

- HOW TO SELECT A PROFESSIONAL LANDSCAPING COMPANY

- *Don't choose a Realtor until you read this important information…*

- 5 Reasons You'll Love Our Service

- 7 Reasons to Call (Company Name) Before Calling Any Other Company

- 3 Reasons…

- 5 Reasons…

- 7 Reasons…

- 10 Reasons…

- 5 Ways to…

- How to Protect Yourself Against…

- Top 10 Reasons to… (do whatever you do) Now!

2. Phenomenal Body Copy

Your body copy is the core message that makes the case you want to make. Here are some principles for creating this part of your message:

- Engage the audience. Remember who you are speaking to (suspect, prospect, or customer/client), make your content relevant and specific to them. If in a live audience, get them to answer questions, raise their hands, stand up, or something that engages them. In an ad, use personal, everyday conversation. Possibly the most powerful word you can use in advertising is "you." And if you can merge their actual name, it's even better! This is why you see marketers use your name in the subject line of an email.

- Get emotional. Customers *always* buy on emotion. They justify with logic. Emotion motivates, not information. Their response is based on how they *feel*. Charge the copy with emotion, not just dry information. See the following Thirteen Most Powerful Words in Advertising.

- Benefits. Be sure to communicate in terms of what your product or service *does* for them, not just what it is. What are the benefits to them?

- Lots of content is okay. You may have learned or assumed that it is not good to put too much information in an ad. In advertising, the more you tell, the more you sell (it's just the opposite in sales). Those who are interested in what you are offering want more information. And you don't want to leave something out that may motivate them to act. Remember, we aren't talking about face to face here. When face to face, you want to limit the amount of information you give, and ask questions.

- Build the experience. Much of the copywriting you may do will be for newsletters, articles, and things of that nature. You have the opportunity to build on your UEP™ (Unique Experience Proposition).

- Use testimonials and endorsements. Real words from real clients and endorsements from highly influential people is some of the best copy you can use. I work with the Zig Ziglar Corporation which is the most trusted name in the training industry. I have a video with Dr. John C. Maxwell, the world's number one leadership expert. These are both examples that build credibility.

- Use the 13 Most Powerful Words in Advertising. The following words are said to be the most powerful words in advertising. It's easy to see why.

  1. Discover (This word is experiential in nature.)

  2. Easy (Everyone wants easy today.)

  3. Guarantee (No one wants to be stuck with something they're unhappy with.)

  4. Health (Everyone wants to be healthy.)

  5. Love (There's an emotional word for you.)

  6. Money (This is important to everyone).

  7. New (You see this one used by Madison Avenue constantly!)

  8. Proven (This word demonstrates they aren't going to be the guinea pig!)

  9. Results (This creates social proof, which is very important.)

  10. Safety (What's the opposite of safe? Danger!)

  11. Save (Everyone is interested in saving time, money, or energy.)

  12. You (This is the most powerful word in advertising according to my good friend and marketing consultant David Frey.)

13. FREE (People say there's no free lunch, but watch them line up for free stuff!)

- Create a sense of urgency. To motivate your audience to action, you must create a sense of urgency. This may be using an expiration date for an offer, a limited supply, or simply the loss factor that occurs by not taking action. For example, if you want to start saving money now, get this product before the offer expires on...." In this simple example, the benefit is saving money (and depending on how much you can share, you want to go deeper with the benefits of saving money). The sense of urgency comes in when you realize you are paying too much now. When? Now. And of course you must act before the expiration date. There are many ways to create a sense of urgency. I recommend that you understand how to do that in your message.

3. A Phenomenal Call to Action

Many sales messages and presentations fall short because there is no call to action. What do you want them to do? Call a phone number? Fill out a form? Make a specific change in their lives? Make sure you tell them exactly what to do and how to do it. Example: Go to this Website right now and get your free CD!

Phenomenal Internet Marketing

In the small business world, some small business owners aren't up to speed on what's happening online. At the same time, some of the younger business owners seem to think that everything should be digital. They dismiss anything offline as old-school, slow, and ineffective. The truth is in the middle (as usual). How *you* use the Internet to market your business really depends on your business and your target market, but here are seven minimum steps to follow.

1. Have at least one Website

Your main site is your "branding" site. In other words, this tells your story. Remember a brand is nothing more than what people say when you are not around. Guess who manages that? You do! Your brand has to come through loud and clear on your site. The first thing people do today when they learn about you is go to your site.

Will they fall in love? Will they run? There is no telling how much damage is being done to small businesses because of horrible Websites. If a customer comes to your site and finds something old and tired, guess how they think about your business. You may not need the flashiest site around, but your image does need to be positive. Since you want to have fresh content, you may consider having a platform where you or someone else can post regular updates or have a social media plug-in.

2. Have an opt-in

A huge mistake I see many small business owners make is not having an opt-in on their Website. An opt-in is a way for prospects to give you their email addresses so you can communicate with them. Offer something free that will benefit them (see the Free Trial Offer for examples). Don't ask for more than the first name and email address at first, because many who visit your site may not be ready to give you a lot of information yet. So, just a contact page isn't good enough. You are asking for too much information without any return for them.

Have a compelling opt-in that offers a solution to your target market's biggest problem. "Sign Up for Our Free Newsletter" isn't compelling enough unless you tell then what the benefit of getting the newsletter is. On my main site, I offer free business building tips by email, free videos, and webinars. I ask only for the first name and email address. But once the person clicks submit, he or she is taken to a page that offers something more valuable. At the time of this writing I am offering a free CD that would be mailed. The audio program reveals the "5 Secrets of a Phenomenal Business." If your business isn't very phenomenal and you want it to be, then you'll order that! And we did get many opt-ins for the free CD program. There are many things you can offer, but the key is to get something prominently posted on your site.

To take that up a notch, have an auto responder (an automatic system that automatically sends an email response to each opt-in immediately). You can customize this to say whatever you want it to say. And if you want to take it into the stratosphere to "Planet Phenomenal" you can create a series of responses over time that brings them step by step to the sale, or takes them through a learning path. By the way, this can be done for every product or service that you provide at every level. It can be as sophisticated as you want. I won't recommend specific programs here because by the time you read this, it could be outdated. But there is no shortage of programs to choose from. This brings me to the next part of your Phenomenal Internet Marketing System.

3. Have a regular outgoing email newsletter

An email newsletter that adds value to your prospects and clients is a powerful tool. As you give them solutions to their problems and offer solutions that your competitors aren't even talking about, you position yourself as the "go to" person in your industry.

4. Have a strong social media presence

At this point, in most cases, it's not whether you should use social media or not, it's which one(s) to use, and how to use them effectively. The way I see social media is like a worldwide networking group that's happening 24/7. Remember that all of business is about relationships. Using social media can help you build and deepen relationships.

Ironically, as I was writing this section, I was on the Sunshine Coast of Australia, overlooking the ocean from my balcony and I had my Facebook page open. I was communicating with people all around the world, and a business associate noticed I was in Australia and contacted me for lunch. Three hours later we were having lunch and set up a business deal. Remember that networking and engaging people on social media doesn't mean you are just going after business deals. You are building relationships that may *become* business deals.

Use the social media platforms that your clients and referral sources are using. Instead of picking the one you like, find out where they are and plug in. Social media doesn't need to own your life either. Once you get familiar with posting, simply make a post once or twice a day (depending on your business and the platform). Always respond to comments, acknowledge retweets, etc. The key is engagement. Don't over promote. Remember, it's about building relationships.

5. Understand SEO

Search Engine Optimization (SEO) is optimizing your Website so that search engines rank it as a superior site for keywords and terms. Most small businesses want to be number one on Google and most marketers and business consultants will tell you that's where you want to be. I'm going to be a little controversial here and say it may not be the most important thing in the world, and it is *not* required to be successful in business.

If you are putting all your effort into SEO and not marketing to your past clients, in most businesses, I would say you have your priorities mixed up. Think and strategize before putting time and energy into SEO that you could be putting into building powerful referral sources. And by all means *do not respond to the spammers* and telemarketers trying to sell you SEO services. Get a referral. And don't do it yourself if it is going to take you away from more important things.

6. Understand paid online advertising

When it comes to Google Adwords, banner ads, and such, follow the guidelines in Phenomenal Direct Advertising and make sure you understand what your plan is! Do *not* get into the world of paid advertising without studying and understanding it. That's kind of like showing up to a gunfight with a dull pocket knife!

7. Use a branded email address

When you are communicating with people, use an email address that has your branding domain in it. Example: howard@howardpartridge. com. Using a Gmail, AOL, or Yahoo email to communicate with business associates devalues your brand. Having your Website address present encourages people to visit your site. Also, have at least your contact info in your email signature (address, phone, Website, etc.), and maybe even an opt-in and a photo.

Phenomenal Direct Sales

Finally, there's the age-old idea of actually making a sales call! Part marketing and part sales, direct selling is when you market directly to a prospect in person. Don't discount this process! When you think of network marketing (also known as multi-level marketing), this is really direct selling.

The fact that you are taking the time to speak to *one* person is not the issue, it's what can happen as a result. In the case of network marketing for example, this person could build a huge team for you in the future. Perhaps it's a person who can become a monthly recurring client for you. My wife is in radio advertising sales. Outside of calling on ad agencies that she is assigned to, she has to actually *call* on someone! Imagine that!

If landing a client is worth the time investment of calling on someone in person, by all means do it. But do it well. And please consider the options I have shared with you so far before investing too much time in this process unless you have already developed a phenomenal system for it. In other words, you could invest the same amount of time with a referral source who can send you as many end-user clients as you want as it takes to land one end-user client. Also, make sure you have done your client-based marketing before investing too much time developing this process.

Many companies have direct sales people and do very well with this. Others, not so good. I get sick thinking about all the time that is wasted by inept sales people. People walk in our office every day selling insurance or business products of some kind. The entertainment begins as we watch them drive up. The other day, the first thing one of them did was open his car door and spit a big hocker right on the parking lot! What a great first impression! He walked in the door and asks, "Is the owner in?" How lame!

This pitiful scenario repeats itself over and over every day. These poor guys obviously haven't been trained well (or at all). Most of them end up quitting, I'm sure. If they are successful, it's completely by accident. I don't know about you, but I don't want my success to be by accident! Many small businesses don't realize that they are failing because of a flawed system. Any strategy that has a chance of working has to be implemented properly. If an account is worth calling on, they are worth investing in.

So, here's what you do…

Walk in with the Secret Weapon (chocolates, doughnuts, candy, or whatever). If you are calling on a lot of people who may or may not be prospects and you can't afford to invest five bucks a call, then use this inexpensive technique: get some clear cellophane baggies with a ribbon from a package supplier. Put four or five pieces of regular candy inside and attach a business card.

Walk in and give it to the rejectionist (I mean receptionist!) and say, "Hi, I'm <your name>, and I brought you some chocolates." She blushes, and you say, "What is your name?" She responds as she tries to gain her composure. "Well, Betty, our company is the most respected, experienced <whatever you do> in the area, and I just wanted to drop by and give you all a free gift <your free trial offer>. Who would I need to talk to about that?"

How hard is that? The candy generates the permission you need to intrigue them with your free trial offer. That gives you the permission to share your UEP, and if they take the free trial offer, you get a presentation! If your presentation is any good and they are truly prospects, not suspects, you are now simply measuring time invested with closing rates. To be effective in direct selling, you first have to give them a compelling reason to meet with you.

Focus on becoming an asset to them and building a relationship. When you get an appointment, offer them your Sales Presentation (next chapter). If you don't, get the decision maker's card and put that person on a follow-up system in Send Out Cards and develop a follow-up system.

The Five M's of a Phenomenal Marketing Plan

Now that you have an idea of the kinds of systems and strategies that are required for a relationship-based marketing system that can create record sales and profits for your business, you need a focused plan. Remember GPS? Well, you can apply GPS to marketing as well. Your sales goal, your marketing plan, and your marketing systems.

An easy way to think about your marketing planning is to use the 5 M's of Marketing. The five M's are:

1. *Money*: What is your sales goal, and how much are you going to invest in marketing?

2. *Mission*: What is the experience you're delivering?

3. *Market*: Who wants that experience?

4. *Message*: What's the message that resonates with them?

5. *Methods*: What systems and strategies will you implement to accomplish the goal?

The First M: Your Phenomenal Money

The first thing you want to have in your plan is a *money* goal. For now we will focus only on the sales and profit goals. Sure, you could have some other objectives such as market share, creating new products, etc., but this simple plan is about taking action, not having a robust, strategic marketing plan that you would take to a bank for funding. This is a bare bones guide that small business owners can easily remember and follow.

Determine what your sales goal is for the next 12 months. If you have history, go back to see how much you did last year. Are you on a growth path? Are sales declining? What significant changes are taking place that can change those numbers? Once you have your annual sales goal, break it down by the month, by the week, by the day, and by the hour. My brother owns a McDonald's, and his profit is determined by how the staff cost is managed by the hour. If you don't have daily or hourly transactions, then break your sales goal down by the smallest measurable increment possible. If you do a few large projects per year, then determine how many projects you are going to do and what the average project amount will be. If you sell products, how many products will be sold at what average price point?

You will also want to break down your sales goal by profit center (or service category) and even by how much you will do in repeat business, referral business, and direct sales and advertising. You will learn about this in Phenomenal Administration Systems.

To get to your sales goal, you will need to know what your *profit* goal is. It all starts with your net profit because that is what funds your life goal. Remember the one and *only* reason your business exists is to be a vehicle to help you achieve your life goals. If the financial spoke on the Wheel of Life is suffering, then everything else in your life will suffer. A business without a profit is just a hobby! I don't know about you, but being broke and in debt isn't any fun. To top it off, working 24/7 to be broke and in debt is even worse! If you're going to be broke, you might as well stay home. At least you could enjoy yourself while you are going broke!

The wonderful thing about being a business owner is that you can plan what you want your profit to be. Of course, Lord willing. None of us know what challenges life will bring us, but we would also be fools to build something without a plan. So we plan and we work the plan the best that we possibly can. The amazing thing is that when you plan and stay focused, many times it works!

Determine what you want your profit to be. Then you will have to determine your cost of doing business (see Phenomenal Administration Systems). Also determine how much you are willing to *invest* in marketing. This should be in your 12 Month Cash Flow Budget. Decide in *advance* what you are going to invest. This will keep you from becoming a victim of the advertising wolves in sheep's clothing. They have an irresistible offer that you are absolutely convinced will work (although it hasn't been proven).

Meanwhile, you aren't doing the proven things that are outlined in this book. A marketing investment amount that includes exactly how much you will invest in each system, strategy, and ad will keep you focused rather than reacting to circumstances. Far too often marketing is done in purely an opportunistic manner rather than a focused plan.

Another thing I have learned from the countless surveys we have taken from small business owners we coach is that there isn't nearly enough invested in marketing. When you see the puny line item called marketing on an income statement, there's no wonder there isn't any business!

You have to plant a seed to get a crop! As the late Jim Rohn said, "You can't say to a field, give me a crop and then I'll plant a seed. You can't say to a fireplace, give me heat and then I'll give you some wood!" It's ridiculous, yet that's what I see every day.

Decide in advance what you are going to invest in marketing. Commit to that investment. Don't make the investment based on whether you have "extra" money or not. Put it in the budget. Make the investment! I know that planning and budgeting doesn't sound like much fun, but it can make you wildly wealthy, which means you can go have all kinds of fun!

How much do you invest in marketing? Whatever it's going to take to get the profit number you need. You may need to do some research on this, but once you line out the things you are going to implement, figure out how much those items will cost. To get this exactly right, you will have to go back and forth on your 12 Month Cash Flow Budget.

The Second M: Your Phenomenal Mission

In Chapter 2, I shared the importance of your *mission*. When it comes to marketing, you want to keep in mind what you are actually delivering. If you have not determined what your mission is, you should come to terms with that before planning your marketing. The reason is that it will determine who your target market is and what your marketing messages will look like.

And keep in mind that if you aren't passionate about the mission you are on, you won't promote it well and you won't lead others to carry it out either.

The Third M: Your Phenomenal Market

Have you determined who your prime target niche *market* is? Everyone is not your customer. If you try to be everything to everyone, you won't be anything to anyone. Not anything significant anyway. You must understand your target market. The more you know about them, the more successful you can be in marketing to them.

Who can benefit from the mission you are delivering? For example, my target market is small business owners who are doing over $100,000 and less than $5 million per year. They have been in business for more than three years, and they feel like slaves to their businesses. They are ready for a solution and probably seeking that solution. They are people who are interested in growing or getting unstuck, and they are teachable.

Of course many other people can benefit from my work. My inspirational teachings have impacted the youth of some of my clients, which thrills me; and some new businesses have enough foresight to realize they need to build it right now instead of later. Network marketers who understand that they have a real business can also benefit. Large corporations can totally utilize our marketing, sales, and leadership systems and have a huge impact; but we don't intentionally target these groups because our focus would be diluted.

It's okay with me if people outside of my core niche want to learn from me, so if you fit one of the other categories, come on in! We can help you! My systems can help any type of business, practice, and even non-profit organizations. But when I market, I am thinking about small business owners who feel like slaves to their businesses. That's my niche target market.

So you want to start by going deep in a niche. You want to become a BIG FISH in a small pond rather than a minnow in a huge ocean. When you are the bomb to that niche, you can have all the business you want and you can literally have people standing in line to pay you the highest prices for what you do. I know because I've done it more than once.

Who is the niche market that desperately needs what you have?

My friend and small business consultant Ellen Rohr says, "Picture your favorite customer—you know, the one who pays your price (and pays on time!). The one you love working with." Those are your perfect niche clients. Do you have a picture in mind? What are their frustrations? What is the competition doing to frustrate them? (I think about Southwest Airlines taking advantage of the ridiculous baggage fees that some airlines are charging. Southwest started advertising "Free Checked Baggage"!)

What is their lifestyle? With whom do they associate? Where do they live? How much money do they make? How old are they? How long have they been in business? Multiple locations or single location? Retail or wholesale?

Do you see how we could fill an entire book just with questions on how to know your niche market? One of the most important questions is how they buy. This will be vital when you get into "Methods" in a moment.

The 4th M: Your Phenomenal Message

Once you determine how much *money* your business needs to produce, what your *mission* is, and who your target *market* is, you now want to craft a *message* that resonates with them. Go back to the "5 Point UEP" (Unique Experience Proposition). This will become the core of your message. You should be able to expand and contract this message based on the situation and the *method* of marketing you are using.

If you are at a networking group that gives you 60 seconds, you can use the full 5 Point UEP™. If you are writing an ad, or you are doing a sales presentation, you'll need to expand the five points. It is also vital to understand how to write marketing copy.

The Fifth M: Your Phenomenal Methods

The final M in your plan is your phenomenal *methods*. What methods of marketing will you use to reach your phenomenal target market? You can have plenty of money to invest, a powerful, passionate meaningful mission, a clearly defined target market, and a compelling message that sells like crazy, but if your perfect prospect never sees it, what's it worth?

What methods will best deliver the message they need? In order to determine this, we must ask ourselves a few questions. How does your prime target market buy services? Online? Offline? Through ads, direct mail, radio, television, newspaper? Do they read trade magazines? Are there online forums where they hang out? Do they primarily buy through referrals? If so, who do they trust? Who has a relationship with them?

I have seen too many small business owners who have a great product or service, but they struggle because they are using the wrong media. Understanding how your perfect target market buys is vital to choosing the right method to reach them.

I hope this chapter has given you lots of ideas on what methods to use. In most small businesses, the simplest, most effective way is to use my referral marketing system of identifying potential referral sources, bring your phenomenal message about your phenomenal mission to them, and inspire them to talk about you to their clients (your perfect target market).

Once they refer, you then have a phenomenal client-based marketing system using something like Send Out Cards that compels them to come back to you and to refer you. I have found that companies that learn how to use referral marketing and client-based marketing well can be very successful without direct advertising or direct sales. I had dinner with an SEO guy not too long ago and he was telling me about the client he helped get to number one on Google. But the guy is still struggling financially. He doesn't have enough business. I could clearly see that in his industry, all he has to do is begin developing a relationship with powerful referral sources. He also is not marketing to his past clients. Big mistake.

I cannot stress enough the importance of a phenomenal referral marketing system and a phenomenal client-based marketing system! Couple that with a phenomenal mission and message—and you have a winning combination!

Chapter 6

Phenomenal Sales Systems

Sales is everything you do to convert prospects into paying customers. *Phenomenal* sales converts the highest number of qualified prospects into customers. A phenomenal sales *system* is a group of working parts that *duplicates results consistently.*

It is very sad to see so much work go into marketing, only to see the sale blown. Small business owners must understand that the sale is *not* automatic (even when you deliver the perfect prospect in your marketing). You've got to make sure your sales process lives up to your marketing efforts.

A few years ago, on a Saturday afternoon, my wife and I were in the market for our son's first car. As I was browsing a local Honda dealer's Website, I noticed a contact form on the site. I put in my phone number and they called me in less than two minutes. I was impressed.

The woman who called was very professional and courteous and invited me to visit the dealership the same day. Once I arrived, I was told that the person I spoke to over the phone was in the "Internet Department" and did not actually talk to the customers at the dealership. *Okay, fair enough,* I thought to myself.

At that point, the worst sales process you can imagine began. These folks had phenomenal marketing, but their sales department needed help! I bought a brand-new Honda, but not from that dealership. Because their marketing didn't work? No, because the salesperson wasn't trained. You must train yourself in sales and you must train your people.

When you work hard to generate a prospect or client, don't get lazy when it comes to sales and service! This is where you are going to prove that your marketing message was true. International branding expert and number one *New York Times* best-selling author Dr. Joseph A. Michelli, says, "A brand is nothing more than what people say about you when you're not around." In essence, your brand is your reputation. If you make a good impression in marketing, you've got to confirm it once you generate a prospect.

Avoiding the Silent Kiss of Death

Every day small businesses are suffering from what I call the "silent kiss of death." The silent kiss of death is when a prospect tries to do business with a company and the owner doesn't even know it! If someone calls your company during business hours and gets voicemail rather than speaking to a person, you're taking a chance of losing that prospect. Many prospects (like me) will hang up and forget about it or call someone else. It doesn't matter if you have Caller ID. By the time you call me back I'm probably off to other things.

If I walk into your store or restaurant and no one is there to greet me, guess what? Some customer types are going to turn around and walk right out. The sad thing is that many times these are the types of clients you want. People who are decisive.

I was reading one of John Maxwell's books, and he shared a story about a time when he and Margaret were in the drive-thru at Krispy Kreme. They love Krispy Kreme when they're hot, but when they drove by the "hot light" wasn't on. They decided to drive through anyway; and to their surprise, the doughnuts were piping hot. When he asked the person at the window why the light wasn't on, she replied, "We get too busy when the light is on, so I didn't turn it on."

If you're like me, I can't imagine how people could think that way, but they do. And it is up to us to train our people. We must train them why it is important to capture as many customers as we can when things are hot. This gets us through the lean times.

Profitable sales cure all other business evils. We need to close as many sales as possible because we are not only squandering the time, energy, and money that was invested in marketing, but we also want to make sure we have reserves for the "evils" that come our way—when we have to pay more tax than planned, something gets damaged, an employee costs us money, someone doesn't pay his bill, the economy tanks, or any other number of things that are completely out of our control. As my friend and author of *The Facts of Business Life* Bill McBean says, "Planning is not predicting the future, it's preparing for it."

Have a Phenomenal Greeting

When people walk into your practice, your store, your restaurant, or call your company, you want to have an enthusiastic greeting that demonstrates you are excited to hear from them. And you should be!

So have a phenomenal greeting when people enter your facility or call your company.

I learned from Zig Ziglar many years ago to answer the telephone with "It's a great day at..." Of course you might want to update that to "It's a phenomenal day at..." (smile). Remember that your callers make several important assumptions about your company when they call.

They are listening to confirm that you will live up to the marketing message. They are making judgments about the value of your service, whether you know what you are doing, and whether you can be trusted or not. When the telephone is not handled properly, you can needlessly create a negative impression that now has to be overcome.

More telephone answering tips:

- Speak slowly and clearly. Your caller may not be listening closely.

- Never answer with "hello" (even your cell phone). A friend may have given a prospect your cell phone number (and why do we answer so negative when it is a family member?).

- Never allow a child or a family member answer your business phone unless they are properly trained.

- Never, *ever* answer with "Can you hold please?" This tells callers they are not important.

- Be upbeat and positive *always!*

- You may want to use a mirror. A smile comes through the phone.

- Eliminate background noise, music, dogs, kids. This can be distracting and takes away from the experience for the client.

- Ask the caller his or her name, write it down, and use the name from that point on.

Sellin' Ain't Tellin'

Do you know about the power of the question? Did you know that "tellin' ain't sellin'"?

Have you heard that asking questions during a sales presentation is much more effective than talking about your product or service? Have you noticed that most sales people break that rule on a regular basis? The last time you bought something, did the sales person ask good questions or did he or she do most of the "telling"?

What about you? How are you doing in that area? Have you practiced the skill of asking questions? Have you discovered the power behind asking the right questions? In fact, have you discovered the right questions to ask for your industry? Would you be surprised to find out that the questions are very similar for any product or service?

What are the best questions to ask?

What about asking a new prospect:

- "Who do I have the pleasure of speaking with today?" (By the way, have you heard that someone's name is music to their ears?) Wouldn't it be a good idea to use their name along with all of the following questions that are directed toward them?

- "How were you referred to us?"

- "What prompted you to call us instead of someone else?"

- "What did (the person or company that referred them) say about us?"

- "What was it about the ad, letter, etc. that got your attention?"

Do you think asking those questions might give you insight into their reasons for choosing you? You don't want to miss that, right? What if you followed that with, "Would you mind if I share a little bit about how we do things here and how we can be of benefit to you?"

What if you then took about 60 seconds to share how you help them solve the major challenges that you know they have based on your industry research? Do you think this might help you connect with them emotionally and to position yourself as the credible source? Have you crafted a compelling UEP™ (Unique Experience Proposition) that will accomplish that? Is it memorized or written somewhere you can access it whenever you speak to a prospect?

What if you then followed that with a series of pre-planned questions that would not only help you discover their needs, but also help them discover what their true needs are? Did you know that most people don't really understand what their true need is and how not solving it is hurting them worse than they realize?

Do you think you could improve the questions you ask? What if you followed the discovery questions with some possible solutions, but you put the solutions in the form of a question? What questions could you follow a statement with? What about, "Does that make sense?" Or, "Does that sound like what you are looking for?"

Did you know that by slowing down and asking confirming questions that you can uncover more objections than you would by just running through your benefits?

Do you realize that by getting them to say "yes" throughout the process, that they will be more likely to say "yes" when you share the investment?

What if you could overcome all objections before you quoted the investment? How cool would that be? By the way, what do you do when you get an objection? What if you asked a question? What kind of question? What if you simply repeated the objection in the form of a question? For example, what if when the prospect says, "It's expensive," you simply repeat it in the form of a question: "So you feel the price is too high?"

Does it make sense that when you simply repeat the objection, they are likely to tell you what the real objection is? Have you heard that when you quote the investment, the first person to speak is usually the one who buys? Do you make it a habit of becoming silent after quoting the investment? If not, is it because you simply have not disciplined yourself, haven't understood the importance until now, or is it because you don't believe in your price?

Finally, does it make sense that getting really good at asking good questions will help you sell more? And how will selling more benefit you? Do you now realize that sellin' ain't tellin'? Do you now know that the more *you* tell, the less you sell? Do you now know that the more *they* tell, the more you sell?

Did you notice that there isn't one single statement in this section? Do you know and understand the power of the question?

My Seven Step Sales System

Many years ago, I developed a system that has proven to work in many small businesses around the world. When you understand and apply this system, I believe you can close more sales because I have seen it work many times. Through this system, you will also confirm that you have the right type of prospect, and you will disqualify the price shoppers (sounds nice doesn't it?).

Step 1. Referred By

The purpose of this step is to:

- *Track marketing results.* This is the best time to track marketing results. When you find out what ad they responded to or how they were referred to you, put that information into a tracking system. This way, you will know how many prospects each ad source is producing. And when you track your close rates on a specific source, you can determine whether that source is working well for you or not. If not, you can change the ad or train the referral source. Does the source truly have the attention and trust of your prime target market? These are the questions that will come from tracking how people were referred to you. If you have a facility, ask, "Have you been to our (store, restaurant, practice, etc.) before?" Over the phone, you would say something like, "Have you ordered from us before?"

- *Build rapport.* By discovering more about why they responded to the ad or what the person who referred them said about you opens the door for you to learn more about them. You can then relate to them based on what they say. For example, when they say, "Suzy recommended your product," you say something like, "Great, we love Suzy, and are so glad she referred you. What did she say about us that interested you?"

- *Learn their motivation.* When they share the answer to that question, you may get tremendous insight into why they chose you over someone else. This also gives you tremendous insight into how your prospects make buying decisions, which helps you dramatically improve your marketing. Depending on your industry, you might ask, "What prompted you to call today?"

Finally, you should understand the emotional reasons your prospects call you. What is the irritating problem or the exciting opportunity they are contacting you about? There may be several. Identify what they are and have a list so that during the interview process, you can connect with those.

Step 2. Connect Emotionally

There will most likely be an overarching, broad, big picture emotion that your prospects are experiencing when they first call you. For example, if you do weddings, what kind of emotions are you dealing with? In this case you have a combination of excitement and fear happening all at once! On one hand, the bride is excited about the biggest day of her life, while at the same time gripped by fear that someone or some*thing* could ruin it all.

You may have heard that people always buy on emotion. They justify their purchase with logic, but the sale is really made on emotion. People not only buy things because they *have* to—they *want* to. The emotion of "have to" is to avoid pain; the "want to" is to get gain. One is the emotion of fear of loss (buying insurance), the other is the emotion of desire (getting that new Lexus).

To be phenomenally successful in sales (instead of being an "order taker"), you *must* connect with the dominant emotions your prospects have. For example, what is the dominant emotion when selecting a service company to come into your home? Fear. Are they going to send someone who is trustworthy? Be sure to connect with them with a statement like, "We know there are unscrupulous service companies out there, but we'll help you avoid them by giving you the most phenomenal service experience ever, guaranteed or your money back."

If the dominant emotion is excitement (like when someone arrives at your hotel to begin their vacation), you want to connect with that and be excited for them.

Step 3. Build Credibility

Now it's time for you to:

- Position your company as the company of choice

- Establish trust and believability

- Get your prospects' minds off what they think is most important at the moment

Start this step by asking the question, "Would you mind if I take a moment and share a little about our company and how we are different from other companies?" If you have serious prospects, they will appreciate this step. Price shoppers don't care, they just want a price, and may say something like, "Can you just tell me how much it is?" to which you will respond, "Absolutely, but I will need to ask you a few more questions to determine that." Just because they are short with you and want a price doesn't mean they're a price shopper. They might just be impatient.

Rushing the sales process won't help you or them, but you can acknowledge their sense of urgency and promise that you'll get through it as fast as possible.

As mentioned previously, best-selling author Bob Burg says, "People do business with those they know, like, and trust." Your sales presentation is all about building on these three things. Trust is critical. This step of building credibility is all about trust.

To establish credibility and trust, use the short version your Five Point Marketing Message. You will share that there are five things that set you apart and how those things benefit the person, the prospect. Remember that number one is reputation, which is trust. At this point, keep the five point marketing message as close to 60 seconds as possible.

Step 4. Perceived Problems

The purpose of this step is to:

• Identify the prospect's needs

• Truly understand the person's fears and desires

• Define the "perceived" problem

Every prospect has a "problem." As my new friend Steve McKnight, the number one real estate investing author in Australia, pounded on in the workshops we did together in Australia: "What business is *every* business owner in? The *problem-solving* business!"

What problem do you solve? There are plenty of people who offer the product or service you do, so you've got to drill down to solve the problem they have. Speaking of drill, no one want wants to buy a quarter inch drill bit, they want a quarter inch *hole*. Their problem is they need a hole. They only need a drill bit because they need a hole. If there was a different way to get the quarter inch hole they need, they would not need a drill bit! Your job as a sales professional is to uncover *why* they need a quarter inch hole!

Even if you're selling a private jet to someone who already owns three Lear jets, you are still solving a problem. Obviously, the man's problem is that he does not feel he has enough jets! And maybe he doesn't. You need to find out *why* he wants or needs another jet.

This step is where the sale is truly made because through the power of asking questions, you are going to uncover and identify the prospect's true needs. Many times prospects don't understand their true needs. They know they need a product or service or they want something. They may or may not know what they are looking for and they may or may not know what will best suit them. Also, you may be higher priced or different from what they are looking for, so instead of just throwing your offer out there, you want to be in a position to ask questions.

Being in that position gives you a huge advantage if you know how to ask questions. You can now get feedback. In marketing, you've got to "tell" a lot. You've got to anticipate the objections and try and overcome them in the marketing message. Or, you've got to invite them into a sales situation so that you can have a conversation. In a sales situation, you can now ask questions instead of assuming what the needs and objections are.

This is done with a series of good questions. Remember that you are interviewing the prospect to determine whether your product or service is the right fit for them, and you are interviewing them to determine what their true needs are so you can get them into the right product or service.

Let's imagine for a second that you are selling lawn mowers. Instead of just spouting off the features of all the lawnmowers (leaving the prospect baffled and confused), you would ask a series of questions, like:

- Do you currently own a lawn mower?

- Are you planning on using it yourself, or will other family members use it as well?

- How big is your yard?

- Are there lots of trees?

- Have you thought about what you want in a lawnmower?

Of course you would have many more questions than this, but you can clearly see the difference between what I just did and what most so-called sales people do.

The key here is to ask questions and then *listen.* Have you ever wondered why God gave you *two* ears and *one* mouth?

Step four is all about solving the issue they reveal and it is your point of reference from now on. Follow what they say to you with:

- What I hear you saying is…

- So, it's important to you that…

- Do you mind telling me more about…?

- Is there anything else you would like me to know?

I have found that doing this well can even cause prospects to ask if they can go ahead and buy! Why is that? Because no one else will *listen* to them! They are asking if they can buy from me and I haven't even asked for the sale! They don't even know the price yet! You have to admit, that's pretty doggone phenomenal!

Step 5. Outline Solution

If you have done a good job identifying the emotional needs and desires, you can now offer the right solution. But not too fast. You still don't get to spew your features. Sorry! Instead, what you are going to do in this stage is feedback what they have told you in the interview and confirm that they agree with the solution. Here are some rules to follow in this step:

Be a Consultant.

Approach the sales process as a consultant. You have shared your five point marketing message and positioned yourself as the consultant. You have generated clients rather than customers through experiential and referral marketing. What do consultants do? They ask questions to determine where you are so they can give you recommendations on how to get where you want to go.

A doctor asks about your symptoms so he can give a prescription. A prescription without a diagnosis is malpractice! It is no different for the sales consultant.

Focus on Benefits.

Be sure to focus on benefits rather than features. Features are what the product or service *is*. Benefits are what the product or service *does* for them. My good friend John Braun ran me through an exercise I never forgot, called the "benefit of the benefit." To drill down to the real benefit, you simply ask that question after each benefit.

For example, right now you are reading this book. What's the benefit of this book? It will help you improve your business. The benefit of that? You'll make more money, have less stress, and more free time. And the benefit of that? You will become a happier person! The benefit of this book is a better *life!* Isn't that funny? So use that simple but effective exercise.

Overcome Objections.

Experience teaches us our prospect's biggest objections. If you have not discovered those in your business yet, you need to. For example, when I was teaching in Australia, we presented a Zig Ziglar package that normally sells really well in the states. The problem was that I usually present the product with Tom Ziglar, who is Zig's son and CEO of the company. Tom didn't make the trip because Zig became critically ill the day before we were supposed to leave.

Tom asked if I was up to going alone, which I was honored to do. Unfortunately Zig's health condition worsened, and he passed away while I was in Australia. Although I have sold many Ziglar products on my own, when Tom is in the seminar room, he brings a great deal of validation to the product.

I did well with the sales but not as good as we predicted based on the number of people in attendance. The seminar sponsor quickly picked up on that and asked those in the audience who didn't buy what their reasons were for *not* buying. He uncovered that some people weren't as familiar with Zig Ziglar as we are in the states. They felt perhaps the package was U.S.-based. Objection: will it work for me here in Australia? He uncovered that they felt the price was a little high, and the one that surprised me the most was they felt they didn't have enough time to listen to all the CDs in the package.

Steve and I both knew this package had tremendous value to them and that it was priced at a ridiculously low investment compared to what they could get out of it. So on the plane from Perth to Adelaide, we re-worked the sales presentation, and the next day we sold out in seconds. The only thing we did differently was to bring up the potential objections in the presentation and overcame them.

For example, to overcome the objection that the product was U.S.-based, we pointed out that Zig Ziglar had a worldwide impact on an estimated 250 billion people. We pointed out people in Australia who had been impacted by his work. On the price objection, we simply asked the audience what the outcome of having a proven goals system would be for them. They agreed by having the system they would be able to make more money, have better relationships, less stress, more happiness, and live a more successful life. What kind of *price* can you put on *that?*

Speaking of price, we stressed the 100 percent money back guarantee and even put a specific dollar amount on it. Why? Because we both knew if they used the product, they would reach more of their goals and make more money. There was no question about that. We just needed to present the opportunity in a different way that day. Someone with less intelligence and experience than Steve would have assumed the audiences were not interested in the package, resulting in low sales.

Use Your 5 Point UEP™

As you are going through the solution, connect the solution to your unique reputation, experience, education, systems, and guarantee. For example, if they say, "Last time we used a service company in your industry we got ripped off," you can point back to your unique reputation and guarantee.

If you do bookkeeping and they tell you their sister-in-law is currently handling the books and there is no issue with trust, but she doesn't have a clue what she's doing, you point to your experience, education, and systems.

Get agreement.

Avoid overloading prospects with too much information. Closing the sale too quickly can result in returns. Instead, pause from time to time and ask them if they agree with the solution. You might ask, "Does that sound like what you are looking for?" It is extremely important to do this to make sure you find the right fit. You will overcome many objections by doing this as prospects help you make adjustments. You get the right product or service for them based on their needs. You will also learn by doing this that there are things that should be in your presentation that are not.

Use their language.

To best connect with your prospects, avoid technical language unless you translate it into a benefit that appeals to them. In fact, use their words. If you are selling boats and the prospect calls one boat the "big guy" and the other one the "little guy," use those words. If you need to reposition the "little guy" or the "big guy," you can do that by using the word and renaming it. Example. Let's say you want the "little guy" to appear more valuable, you might say, "Did you know that the little guy has some huge benefits, such as…"

Use their pace.

One of the greatest things a salesperson can learn is the various communication styles humans have. Behavior assessment programs reveal that some of us are generally outgoing or reserved and people- or task-oriented. One of the simple but effective assessments is called DISC.

D = Dominant. This style is outgoing and task-oriented, so they are in a hurry to get things done.

I = Influential. This style is outgoing and people-oriented, so they like to talk.

S = Steady. This style is reserved and people-oriented, so they want to know that you care.

C = Competent. This style is reserved and task-oriented, so they want complete accuracy.

The D style is fast-paced, get-to-the-bottom-line, so you want to speed up. The I style likes to chat it up, so have some fun and lighten up. The S is very loyal, so they want to know that you will be there to support them. Reassure them that you will support the product when they need you. The

C style will have lots of questions, so you want to slow down and give them lots of detail. The D and I style will probably decide fast, whereas the S and C will go slower.

It's a good idea to find out what behavior style you use during the sales process so you can be aware of how you are coming across. If you are an I and you are selling to a C or vice versa, you've got to be aware! Otherwise, you'll blow the sale and not even know why.

Discover Your DISC Communication Style Here
for FREE!

www.howardpartridge.com/DISC

Step 6. Share the Investment

Did you notice this section isn't titled Quote the Price? Rather it is Share the Investment. What's the difference between a price and an investment? A price is something you've got to *paaaay*. An investment gets a return. The best investments get huge returns! The more you invest, the bigger return you get.

A fatal mistake that order takers make is not just quoting a price, but quoting it before the first five vital steps have taken place. Can you now see how the first five steps build the value of the unique experience you offer? You want the value to be so high that when you quote the investment, it sounds like a great value. Build the value of the return higher than the investment.

This doesn't mean that all prospects will automatically buy. They may be hoping to get your phenomenal service experience for the same price other people charge. They may be expecting to pay more, but are surprised how much more it is. That's okay as long as you have a good closing rate (the number of people who buy compared to those who don't).

As the business owner and/or sales consultant, you need to know the ROI of the benefits you provide. It is up to us to be able to communicate that. It doesn't mean that every prospect will accept it right now. They may have to have some experiences before they come to terms with it. Here's an example. In-home service companies such as carpet cleaners, plumbers, air conditioning companies, cable TV companies, and many others are sending technicians into people's homes.

What is the potential cost of someone with a criminal background coming into your home? What is the potential cost of having someone who damages your property and they don't have adequate insurance? What does it cost to fix the problems they create? And by the way, how much is your time worth? If they do a lousy job and you have to spend all of your time trying to correct the problems, you simply wasted your money and your time. So the potential *cost* outweighs the investment.

Never share the investment until...

• You have built the *value* in *excess* of the investment

• They have *agreed* that is what they are looking for!

• Shared how your company is different from *any other* company

• You've shared *exactly* how you are going to solve their problem

To share the investment, simply say, "Mr./Ms. Prospect, your investment today will be…." Once you have shared the investment, don't say another word! Have you ever heard that the first person who speaks after the price is quoted is usually the one who buys? I have found it's pretty much true!

You must understand that something amazing happens when you quote the investment. They leave (in their mind). They go to the justification station in the mind. If you interrupt that process by continuing to talk, they get confused or pressured and may shut down. Or they feel pressure to buy, which turns into a return for you later on. They get what's called buyer's remorse.

Instead, *zip it!* After you quote the investment, just be quiet. It will take some people longer than others to justify or reject your offer. That's okay. Just stay quiet. Silence is literally golden in this situation because it can make or cost you *real* money. When they finally speak, they may say yes, or they may give you an objection.

Step 7. Overcome Objections

In the best of situations, you will have already overcome all objections during step five. If not, this is where you will need to apply this skill. Did you notice the word I just used? Skill. To be a phenomenal business owner and sales consultant, you need skill that requires training. Train yourself with information, seminars, and coaching.

When you get an objection, ALWAYS ask a question. ALWAYS!

If there was ever a time when questions were important in the sales process, it is in this step. When you get an objection, always ask a question. Always. What kind of question? Well, what if you simply repeated the objection in the form of a question?

For example, if the prospect says, "Wow, that's expensive!" you say, "So you feel it's expensive?" They now have to respond. Remember the more *they* tell, the more *you* sell. They might just say, "Yes, it's expensive." To which you respond with, "Would you mind sharing what you mean by too expensive?" Your goal is to get more information about their objection.

There are literally hundreds of closing techniques and questions you could use, so I recommend you study Zig Ziglar's Secrets of Closing the Sale

CDs as well as anything else he produced on the subject. Again, you want to develop your skill in this area.

Five Ways to Overcome Price Objections

If you have come all the way to this step, the only objection you should have is "price." Here are my five favorite ways to overcome price objections:

1. Review the value.

The reason you went through the Seven Step Sales System is so you can go back to the agreement points in step five. If you assessed the market correctly and you know that you offer more value for the investment, go back and connect with that. Reconnect them with your five point message. Confirm that they truly want to work with a company that has the unique qualities your company has and that they truly want to get the benefits you offer.

Perhaps they are convinced they can get "the same thing" somewhere else. Obviously, you didn't convince them of the uniqueness of your product or service and the value, so you now must do that.

Get their permission to explore the other options with them. For example, let's say they are buying a service, and they have used your competitors in the past. Ask them why they didn't call that company to start with? Why have they called you? Perhaps you will find out that the other company can't service them when they need to, or they've gone out of business, they can't remember their phone number, or whatever.

You can now ask a question like, "Why do you think that is?" In other words, perhaps they can't service you or they went out of business because they didn't charge enough. The question is, "Do you want to have a company that you can rely on over and over again?"

If they are comparing you to another competitor that charges a lower price, you want to ask questions that will cause them to wonder what the other company is leaving out. What is their true reputation? What kind of experience do they really have? Are they really trained? Can they really and truly deliver the experience you want? And do they stand behind their work?

If you are telling me they can do all of this for a cheaper price and there is nothing different, you better get scheduled with them quickly before they go out of business! I mean really, isn't that just the plain truth? You know it and I know it. You get what you pay for, and companies that charge too little cannot deliver consistently for very long.

You must create contrast between you and them, and create doubt without mentioning any competitor by name. And you must attract the kinds of prospects in your marketing that you have a chance to close. Don't try to sell a KIA customer a Mercedes, and don't try to sell a Mercedes client a KIA!

2. Offer payment options.

If you haven't determined what their budget is (if they have one), you want to do that now. Depending on your industry, you may want to put that in the interview process in step four. If not, when you get a price objection, ask, "What were you planning on investing in this project/product?" If they don't know, it means they don't have a basis for judging the pricing. They probably haven't been shopping.

At this point, you have a couple of options. If you can get them to give you a figure, try this option. Let's say the investment is $500 and they didn't want to spend more than $350. You say, "How would it be if you could put the three fifty down today and pay the rest later?" My experience has been that if they really want your product or service (and that is the key: building desire in the presentation), they will find a way to pay for it if they don't feel they can afford it today.

Of course you want to mention that you accept major credit cards. Although I don't like to help people get into debt, and I'm a big fan of Dave Ramsey (Dave helps people get out of debt), I do allow people to use credit cards to pay for my products and services (Dave doesn't). If I was in Dave's business, I'm sure I would only allow debit cards like he does.

If they want your product, work with them on the payment options by first determining how much they can put down today. If you can cover your hard costs on the first installment, you haven't lost anything even if they never pay you. If they don't buy, you may have lost a client forever. So, my goal is to close today. If you are convinced your product or service will really help them, you should have a strong desire to close as well.

3. Referral Reward Program.

Another strategy is to show them how they can get their entire investment back by using your referral reward program. Simply ask, "Did you know you can get all of your money back with our referral reward program?" Share how the program works and how they get their money back. For example: "Mrs. Prospect, we offer a 10 percent referral reward for any new client you send us. That means that once you have sent just ten new clients, you will have gotten all of your money back on this project." I have found that some people who truly can't afford my product or service, will work extra hard at getting referrals for me so they can get my service. Again, it's about creating desire for your product.

4. Down sell.

With this strategy, you will offer a lower priced product or change the scope of the project. You settle for less money today, but you did not lower your price! If you lower your price without attaching it to a condition, you lose all credibility! In their mind, you could have offered the lower price to start with. Keep in mind that people will ask for a lower price simply because they know many salespeople will immediately drop the price. Don't do it if you want to maintain trust.

Let's say you are selling fitness training. You have presented the value of a package that includes X number of weeks in group training and a few one-on-one sessions. You could take out some of the sessions. You are still selling training at a profitable rate, just settling for a lower package today.

5. Offer a free trial.

In the marketing chapter, I revealed the Free Trial Offer Program. Not only is it a phenomenal marketing tool, it can also be a phenomenal closing tool. Many times your prospects don't know how to value your product or service and they can't imagine how good it is. Therefore, allow them to experience it for free if you can. If you can't actually give them a sample, create some sort of experience that allows them to see and feel exactly what it will be like.

Also in the marketing chapter I talked about the "free ride" Lexus gives its prospects. Chick-fil-A was the first to offer free samples in the mall. Now everyone does it. If you have a cleaning company for example, offer to clean an area free as a sample. If you have a high-value product or service, you may want to borrow a tactic from the time-share industry. Have you ever been on vacation and noticed a little booth or office that advertises a free resort stay or a free jet-ski rental? In order to get the freebie, you have to listen to a 90-minute presentation. And guess what? It works! Of course you'll leave out the high pressure that some of those outfits use.

Creating a Sense of Urgency

In the marketing chapter, I briefly covered that you need to create a sense of urgency in your message. In marketing, you create a sense of urgency to respond. In sales, you also need to create a sense of urgency to close.

The reason is that the level of desire can wane after the presentation is over. The emotion dissipates. Remember that all sales are made on emotion. Some prospects will not close right away, and understanding the behavior styles and when to close or not will be part of your ongoing training. One technique you can use in those cases is to go ahead and do the paperwork, but put it on hold until a certain date.

It goes like this. "Mr. Prospect, I understand that you want to think about it. At the same time, I know you've expressed interest in the special offer, correct?" "What if we do this...let's go ahead and do the paperwork, and we'll put a hold on it for you so you will have time to think about it. If you decide not to move forward, we'll shred the paperwork. How does that sound?"

I have seen this work many times. Your testing will show how many end up cancelling and how many don't. By the way, you then work on a suitable date (not next month!) and you put a date on the paperwork and ask about processing the payment tomorrow (or whenever it is) if you don't hear from the prospect. You want to avoid having to track down the person. Put the follow-up responsibility on the prospect. Remember once more: if your product or service benefits the person, there is no harm in working hard to help!

How to Double Your Profit with the Most Profitable Sale Ever!

In any business there is one type of sale that brings the most profit. There is one single sales activity that can make the most difference in the profitability of your company. *Not taking advantage of this all-important sales opportunity will cost you thousands of dollars.*

The most profitable sale ever made is called the "up-sell" or "add-on" sale. Why is it the most profitable sale ever? Because you have already invested the time, money, and energy acquiring and serving your client. Therefore, anything that is added to the "ticket" is extremely profitable. This makes the up-sell sale the most profitable sale you can make.

Why Most Small Business Owners Don't Up-Sell

Have you been guilty of not making the up-sell in the past? I have. Why is that? Here are the reasons I have found that up-sells aren't made (by the owner *and* staff):

1. Pushy salesperson

You don't want to appear as the "used car salesman" stereotype. I will share with you in just a moment that you are actually doing your customer wrong by not offering the up-sell. I will prove it to you and you will agree, so stay with me.

Our view of a salesperson has likely been skewed as we grew up. We have been conditioned to believe that all salespeople are con artists. Maybe we grew up seeing salespeople take the discretionary income from our families. You must see yourself as a consultant who is looking out for your clients.

2. Fear

Somewhere along the way we have picked up the fear of rejection and we don't really know where it comes from. When we get confidence through sales training, we have goals, we have a system that we follow, and we have the desire to reach our goals and take the best care of our clients, we can have the focus to move forward even in the midst of fear.

Do you remember the acronym for FEAR? False Evidence Appearing Real. Your wonderful imagination is creating emotional images. They are almost always false, but appear real because of the way our minds work. Winners don't lack fear, they proceed in the face of it.

3. Lack of training

Sales training gives you confidence. If you have staff, they must be trained in sales and presenting the products and services properly.

4. No system

You should have scripts and procedures that are followed consistently. When you develop the right system that consistently works, it is then up to you to consistently implement it.

5. Lack of goals

If you do not have clearly defined, compelling financial goals, you are less likely to do all you can in this area. It's a human fact. If your life goals don't require money, hopefully the cost to your client will motivate you to make the sale. You may have employees who have not connected their financial position to their future and may have "stinkin' thinkin'" about money. If so, that will limit the possibilities. You need to help them expand their money mindset.

6. Busy

We are all busy today, but let me ask you a question, "If you don't make the most profitable sale ever and spend your time on less profitable activities, isn't it costing you *more* time to *not* up-sell?" Ponder that for a moment.

Not making the up-sell is doing your customer WRONG!

How is it possible that not up-selling is doing your customer an injustice? Let me ask you another question, "If your client doesn't use your extra services, will it *cost* them anything?" If not, you shouldn't be selling it. There is obviously a gain from purchasing your product or service, so there must be a cost if they don't.

Also, if they don't buy it from you and they learn about it from your competitor, how do you feel about that? Are all of your competitors honest and ethical? How do you feel about them taking care of your customer rather than you?

Finally, do you have a phenomenal reputation? Do you have experience? Are you educated in your field and do you educate your clients? Do you provide a phenomenal customer service experience? Do you stand behind your product?

Then wouldn't you agree that if they don't get to take advantage of all you have to offer, you are actually doing them wrong by not at least letting them know about it? It is their decision, but you are the consultant. As advisors, it is our job to share the opportunity with them.

How Much Money Are You Leaving on the Table?

Think about how much you could potentially add to your business each day in add-on sales if you or your people were trained and focused. Now multiply that by five days a week. Now multiply that by 52 weeks per year. Now multiply that by the number of sales or service representatives you have. A mere $100 per day x 5 days per week is $26,000 per year. If I have ten representatives, that's $260,000 per year!

And speaking of staff, I recommend giving them an incentive on the add-on sale. I know there may be some "purists" that disagree, and that's okay if you do. But wouldn't it be nice to give them a "raise" without having to pay more and more just for them to exist? Sooner or later, the business isn't sustainable because we continue to give raises without increasing profits.

How to Make Up-Sells Consistently

First, you must train yourself in sales. This is a worthy endeavor. Get everything you can from the Zig Ziglar Corporation on sales training. Train your staff. Zig always said, "Everyone in the company may not be in sales, but anyone can cost the company a sale!"

And by the way, what if the receptionist asked a question like, "Did you get the XYZ product? It's really amazing!" The receptionist can then help make a sale. That brings me to the next point.

Ask Questions

Remember that selling isn't telling. And telling isn't selling. Determine the additional items you have to offer. In the interview process, include some questions that will reveal the prospect's beliefs about that product or service. Ask questions that bring up that conversation.

Here's an example: The first business I started is a high-end cleaning firm that cares for stone floors, Oriental rugs, and fine textiles. The most profitable and most valuable up-sell is sealer for the stone and fabric protector for the textiles. We built questions into the script such as, "Did you get protector the last time you had this cleaned?" We don't sell it at that moment, instead we gather information (the more they tell, the more you sell).

Later on, during step five, we outline that the solution includes sealer or fabric protector. Not having investment furnishings protected costs the client big time down the road, yet many companies fail to even mention it. The result is the customer's property is at risk and the company doesn't make the profit it could. The owner doesn't reach his or her life goals, which may include passing on some of those profits to a good cause. Can you see how this all fits together in a phenomenal business?

Once you have opened the conversation, ask for permission to share more. Once you get that permission, you can go into a full interview on that particular service or product. If demonstrations or a free trial is appropriate, be sure to offer that.

A final note...don't offer *anything* until you have established rapport with the client and you have secured *believability*. You must establish yourself as a trusted consultant and representative before attempting an extra sale. Many times this is accomplished by WOWing the client with the primary service or product first.

Speaking of service—next up is Phenomenal Operations Systems.

Chapter 7

Phenomenal Operations Systems

Operations is everything you do to serve your clients. *Phenomenal* operations delivers a meaningful service experience that engages, educates, and entertains your clients, making them feel special. A phenomenal operations *system* is a group of working parts that *duplicates results* consistently (without you having to be there).

Michael E. Gerber, author of the E-Myth books says, "Most business owners are not entrepreneurs, they're technicians." If you are like most small business owners, this may be the strongest area in your business, but you might be surprised to find out that being strong in this area is creating your biggest weakness. If you aren't able to duplicate your technical skills, you won't have a system, which means you'll remain a slave to the business.

Chances are you went into business doing what you do because you had skill in that industry. Maybe you worked for someone else, or maybe you knew someone else who was successful in that business. The fatal assumption as Michael Gerber calls it, is to assume that since you're the best pie baker, the best teacher, the best trainer, the best plumber, or whatever it is that you do, that you will be successful in business. Nothing could be farther from the truth. But like the other four areas, this one is just as vital to the success of your business. The question is whether you'll be successful turning your technical expertise into a system.

The Most Phenomenal Service Experience Ever!™

If you want to know what the most phenomenal service experience ever looks like, look no farther than the Ritz-Carlton Hotel Company and their legendary service. One of my best friends, Luis Hernandez, and I go to Puerto Rico together sometimes, and last year I took my mama with us since it was her 75th birthday (yes, when you're from Alabama, it's "mama" not "mom"). I wanted to do something special, so we stayed at the Ritz-Carlton in San Juan.

The staff there literally jumps to attention when a guest is present. They call you by name and make a big deal about you. My good friend Joseph Michelli wrote a book about it called *The New Gold Standard*. In that book, he unpacks the philosophy and the strategies. The Ritz-Carlton has been very successful building a business by providing the most phenomenal service experience ever.

As I write this section, I'm on a remote island on the Great Barrier Reef off Australia. As I was planning the trip, I researched my travel book and looked up the Website of the resort online. The Website was absolutely amazing and the island looked stunning. I booked the trip completely online and any correspondence I had was by email. The confirmation email was one of the best I've ever seen. I took a helicopter from the mainland over to the island so I could see the reef from the air, and the view of the little island among the dots of reef encased in emerald waters was breathtaking. As the helicopter made its slow, rocking descend onto the helipad, I imagined I had arrived at "Fantasy Island" (remember that TV show?).

Excitement swelled up in me as I walked up the little sand path to the reception area. Within five minutes I knew the service experience wasn't going to match the incredible island. The front desk clerk seemed bothered. The more staff I met, they all seemed to have a chip on their shoulders. This was a completely different experience from what I had in the rest of Australia. Almost everywhere I'd been, the people had been super nice. The flight attendants actually smiled and stopped to chat a bit.

But not at this resort. In fact, they didn't even make eye contact. If this was a Ritz-Carlton property, they would have greeted me politely and asked me how I was doing. Because of the incredible beauty of the island and the unique location, they have the opportunity to create the most phenomenal service experience ever. Someone is asleep at the wheel.

You see, there's a difference between providing a functional service and providing the most phenomenal service experience. As stated previously, before I started my first business, I was a waiter. I worked in high-end restaurants where we performed tableside cooking. I wore a tuxedo to work, and each dish that was prepared at the table was flamed as a finale. Back in those days, you could smoke inside. When someone pulled out a cigarette, a lighter was in front of them immediately. We "waited" just far enough away to give them their personal space, but were close enough to anticipate their needs before they occurred. Water or iced tea was topped off before they had to ask for it. We hovered without being a bother. It was the most phenomenal service experience ever.

In this chapter, I want to unpack what this can look like in your business, regardless of what you do. If you're a doctor or dentist, when your patient walks in, you want him or her to have the right experience. If you have a gym, what kind of experience do your members have when they come in? The same goes for a retail store, church, or any organization that wants to make a unique impression.

If you are a service company like plumbing, office equipment repair, telephone systems installation, cable TV, carpet cleaning, air conditioning, or something of that nature, what are the steps of providing the most phenomenal service experience ever?

If you are an independent professional such as an insurance agent, realtor, or sales professional, what are the things you can do to make your clients feel special? We used to have a financial adviser who handled the 401k type of stuff for one of my companies. This guy would come in, sit down, and read the paper. When it was time to get up and speak to our team, he put a chart up on the wall and began to speak what might as well have been Greek. Needless to say, he is no longer with us.

The guy we have now goes out of his way to build a relationship with each employee. Just before Thanksgiving, we received the biggest goodie basket I've ever seen in my life. It was HUGE! Of course it had some Starbucks stuff in it for me (hint), and it had something for every employee. Master stroke.

WIIFM

You may not feel that you are up to providing that level of service experience. You may feel it is beneath you. You may be thinking, *How in the world could I get my staff to act that way?* I'm here to tell you that not only can you change your culture, I want to offer you some benefits of creating a phenomenal service system. Perhaps if we can tune into your favorite radio station, WIIFM (What's In It For Me), you'll be more likely to put the work into making this happen.

What's in this for you:

1. Your clients will be happier, which means you'll have fewer headaches.

2. Your staff will be happier, which means they'll stay longer and work harder.

3. Your service experience will no longer require you to make every client happy.

4. You'll make more money.

Remember the PLV (Potential Lifetime Value) of a client that we talked about in Phenomenal Sales Systems? Before looking at the economic value of a client, let's talk about the fact that they *deserve* to be treated right. Customers deserve a positive, friendly experience at minimum. Customers deserve to be valued for the simple fact that they are human beings who should be highly regarded. That is the minimum standard. God's phenomenal creation standing in front of you!

John Maxwell says when you don't value people, you de-value them. This is the core issue surrounding customer service. How we value people has a direct impact on how we treat them. You can say you value someone, but your actions show the true value. The only reason you need to value your customers is because they deserve it. They pay your bills for you. We should all be grateful for our customers' support. Without them we have nothing.

What You Need to Understand to Put this Together

To create and deliver the most phenomenal service experience ever, you'll need to first understand the emotional state of your niche prospect. When your clients buy your product or service, what is their emotional state? Excitement? Fear? Uncertainty? Pride?

For example, when I arrived on "Fantasy Island," I was very excited because visiting the Great Barrier Reef was on my bucket list. I would be relaxing and writing my book. It would be a special time for me. But because they never connected to that and never took the time to understand, I'll never return.

Imagine you are a wedding consultant. What is the emotion of a soon-to-be-bride? Excitement. But at the same time fear. Fear that someone or something could ruin the most important day of her life. If you don't connect with that and focus just on the product, you are missing a humongous opportunity. In a service business where you are invited into the most private areas of someone's home, do you think there is some fear and uncertainty in homeowners' minds the first time they use your service? You bet there is. And you must connect with it.

A good start to connecting with the emotional state is by following step two in the sales presentation—having a statement that you understand what they are feeling. Now of course if you have gone through the sales process already, you have built some rapport and trust. But if someone walks into your restaurant or your retail store, you must engage them properly.

Recently I walked into a restaurant and I was in a hurry. After a few minutes of no one even showing up at the table, I knew that the rest of the experience would most likely be slow as well, so I got up and left. Keep in mind that this restaurant had been specifically recommended by the hotel. I went straight there without shopping around. Can you see how you can do a phenomenal job marketing and closing the sale, only to have everything fall apart at the service level?

So engage your clients and make them feel like they are the most important people in the world right now. And they are! Your life goals are connected to this vehicle called your small business. If you don't have service, you have nothing.

Speaking of engagement, another big customer service mistake I see on a regular basis is employees engaging with one another, while ignoring the customer. Have you been to a grocery store and the cashier and the bagger are chatting it up and the only thing they say to you is "5.95." Drives me crazy!

I know they haven't been trained, so it makes me want to go and grab the manager. Of course the manager hasn't been trained, so now I want to talk to the owner. Well it's corporate owned and you can't really talk to anyone. This is why small business owners can have more influence in the marketplace than any other man-made institution. We can make a difference in the lives of others! Have you ever been on a flight and the flight attendants are having a phenomenal time together, but when you ask for something, they scowl. Make sure this doesn't happen with your business. Thoroughly train your staff on the mission.

The Mission—Providing Your Unique Service Experience

As discussed earlier, the first vital component of a system is the mission. Your client has a problem and you have a solution. The solution is delivered by providing a unique service experience they can't get anywhere else. Have your employees memorize that mission. Every conversation, every meeting, and every coaching session is in context of your mission.

"The most important thing in any company is its culture."
–Dr. John C. Maxwell

You see, when we accomplish the mission (or not), a culture is developed. A culture is the result of the values we live by and how we act. The culture is built through how we live out our values. You can change your culture by living out different values.

Five Values that Create the Most Phenomenal Service Experience Ever

Do you remember the five things I shared with you in the marketing message earlier? Reputation, Experience, Education, Systems, and Guarantee. What would happen if we thoroughly communicated and trained our staff on how to live out those values? What if we talked a lot about what affects our reputation (positively or negatively)? What if we helped our staff gain more experiences they could pass on to the client and showed them how it helps us accomplish our mission? What if we immersed ourselves in education at every level? What if we had a step-by-step system at every level of the company that was proven to result in clients feeling that they had the most phenomenal service experience ever? What if we actually did what we said when it came to our guarantee?

What a wonderful world it would be! Can you see how training your staff on the same five points you are offering your clients result in exceeding client expectations? We can't say one thing and do another.

How to Make Your Clients Feel Special

Mary Kay Ash built an amazing company culture. She frequently said, "Imagine every human being you meet has an invisible sign around their neck that says *make me feel special.*" Zig Ziglar said, "You can have everything in life you want, if you just help enough other people get what they want." What do your clients want? They want to feel special.

Start by using your client's name. Famous leadership writer and lecturer Dale Carnegie said, "The sweetest sounding music to a person's ear is their own name." By the way, this also benefits you outside of serving your clients. When you begin to recognize others by name, they will respond differently. I travel a great deal and make it a habit to call anyone who serves me by name. Whether it's a flight attendant, front desk clerk, wait staff, or bell hop, I ask them their name if they don't have a name tag. I prefer calling people by their last name if I am serving them, but if you have a casual atmosphere like Southwest Airlines, you might call them by their first name.

I first started calling people by their names so I could get better at remembering names. But I soon realized I got better service when I did that. Instead of having a flight attendant scowl, many times they check with me personally every time they pass by! One flight attendant moved me to first class after the airplane doors were shut (which is illegal post-911). It is amazing to me that such a small thing makes a difference, but it does. It just goes to show you how much people are starving to be recognized. Your clients are no different.

They crave attention. Give it to them and you'll be the star. Recognize them by name.

Also, anticipate their needs. Remember the high-end waiter example? The water was filled before the customer asked for it. We knew someone would pull out a cigarette, so the lighter was ready.

Work is theatre, and every business is a stage.

The Experience Economy book that I mentioned in Phenomenal Marketing Systems has a subtitle: *Work is Theatre and Every Business is a Stage.* A Phenomenal Operations *System* is a theatre production designed to create the right *experience* consistently.

I can't tell you too much about the theatre firsthand because I'm not allowed to go to a show with my wife any longer. That ended about ten years ago because of one simple fact: I fall asleep. Yes, that can be a problem when a lot of money has been spent on tickets and I'm snoring or drooling on some lady's mink! I get up early to write, think, and plan. I drink strong coffee in the morning, and I'm full throttle all day. As soon as I sit down in the evening, I'm out. If we turn on the news or a great movie, it's rare that I'll make it through.

A few years ago, I was working on a joint-venture project with a multibillion dollar company. We were meeting all the "big Whigs" in Las Vegas. My contact called me and told me they were taking us to a show. "Oh…," I said. He responded, "Yes, how did you know we're going to see "O" [a Cirque de Soleil show], aren't you excited?" "Ohhhhhh," I said, thinking to myself, *This is going to be really bad. Here these high-level guys are taking us out for a big dinner and a show, and I'm going to fall asleep! Not good!*

I made sure I had a pocketful of sunflower seeds (I use those to stay awake when I drive). I drank a Venti Starbucks right before the show—but believe it or not, I can go right to sleep after drinking one of those things. I told my friends on the team to make sure I sat as far away from the head guys as possible. And I told my buddy next to me that he had my permission to do *whatever* he had to do to keep me awake.

Fortunately, I found a new solution to my problem. I clapped as hard as I could after every scene. So hard that my hands hurt after the show, but it kept me awake. And the best part was, because of the excessive clapping they all thought I loved the show. Of course that could become a problem if we ever go to Las Vegas together again!

When you think of theatre, what is it? It's entertainment. What does entertainment do? It takes you on an emotional journey. My wife loves the movie *The Sound of Music* partly because it was the first movie she saw at a theatre. What emotion do you want your experience to invoke? Excitement? Concern? Passion?

Remember that customers always buy on emotion. Always. And when you create a phenomenal service experience, you have built in the emotion you want to help your client feel. Let me pause to remind you not to manipulate. You have a responsibility not to cross the line. Using undue pressure or fear is out of line. Make sure that what you are offering and how you present it and serve it is with the utmost integrity—and make sure it's a win for everyone involved.

Now think about this: the "show" is repeated night after night, invoking the same emotion at the exact point in the production each and every time. This is what needs to happen in your business. What does the set look like? This is your store, your vehicles, your materials. Who are the characters? What do they look like? How do they act? What do they wear (the costume)? What is the script? Can you see how creating a system of production is much like a theatre production? It's a show. Treat it that way.

Niche Appeal

Here's a striking statement from *The Experience Economy* book, "Too many workers behave no differently on stage than they do in their private lives." One of my best friends, Jim Bardwell who worked with me as I grew my first company, understands "creating the experience" like few I've ever seen. In my early seminars, Jim often did presentations for me (sometimes in costume!). He used to teach "in the service business, you've got to have universal appeal." In other words, whoever your audience is, your character must appeal to them.

If your clients are conservative, you probably don't want to look like a biker. On the other hand, if you work at Harley-Davidson, that would be an advantage. We live in such a "me" world today, that we don't really think about customer service. And if you think about it, our children really haven't learned how to serve. In a world of instant gratification, where we tap our foot in front of the microwave, they don't really know what service is.

Most likely, they have never had to serve (unless smart parents intentionally had them do so, for which you have my deepest respect). Modern conveniences have eliminated the need for each other in many cases. Many can't help their neighbor with finances because they are just as broke and in debt. If the parent does go to the neighbor's house to help fix a car or cut up a fallen tree, where are the children? Usually playing a video game, talking on the cell phone, or watching YouTube videos. We are creating a generation that doesn't know what service is, so we must be very intentional about teaching it to them.

Make sure your image, scripts, and procedures resonate with your niche target market. Think of Ritz-Carlton again. Their guests are high-profile, wealthy individuals. Can you afford body piercings, sloppy clothing or speech? No. The experience must be created to engage and entertain your target market. If you have a business where it's all about speed and efficiency, then focus on that. Do everything you can to make the entire experience that way. The point is that you must create the experience that will give your perfect niche market what they want—and more.

Customer satisfaction is...worthless!

My friend Jeffrey Gitomer wrote one of the best customer service books ever—*Customer Satisfaction is Worthless. Customer Loyalty is Priceless.* The goal is to create loyalty.

In the book *Raving Fans,* legendary leadership expert Ken Blanchard and co-author Sheldon Bowles featured a loyalty ladder that goes like this:

- *Suspects*—These are people who fit your defined target market, information that you should know as you create your customer service vision. They may or may not become customers. That depends on your *marketing* system.

- *Prospect*—These are people who take some form of action. They visit your Website or come into your store. They may or may not become customers. That depends on your *sales* system.

- *Shopper (or Customer)*—These are people who buy something. They may or may not return, and whether they move up the ladder (or not) depends of your *operations* system.

- *Client*—People become clients when they buy a second time.

- *Member*—Clients graduate to members once they feel they are respected for their business and receive extra care and attention.

- *Advocate*—People become advocates when they are very satisfied with your products and services and tell others about your business.

- *Raving fans*—Someone is a raving fan of your business when they do the "selling" for you. The products and services exceed their expectations and they encourage others to buy.

Your Phenomenal Operations Systems along with your Phenomenal Client-Based Marketing Systems are key to bringing them back to move them up the loyalty ladder.

Creating Your Phenomenal Operations System

In order to create the experience and the system, you need to think about the steps that each customer goes through. Jan Carlzon described how he turned around struggling SAS airlines by creating what he called "moments of truth." Every customer interaction is a moment of truth. *The Experience Economy* book says every time the customer sees an employee, that's a theatre moment, so we have to break down the steps of customer interaction and make sure we are creating the most phenomenal service experience system, step by step.

My good friend and colleague Ellen Rohr has a great way to think about this. Instead, of trying to think about each positive step you want to create from *your* perspective, think about what could go *wrong* from the *customer's* perspective.

She used a restaurant as an example: Get in your car and drive down the road. Now turn around and drive back to the restaurant. What could go wrong as you approach the restaurant? The sign is hard to see. Or it's not lit. Now you approach the door. It's not clean. You step inside and maybe the hostess isn't there. Can you see how imagining what could go *wrong* can give you the steps to take?

Wow. Brilliant!

I recently promoted one of my team members to Operations Manager of my service company. The main point I shared with him was *prevention*. Imagine what can go wrong and be proactive to prevent any level of service issue to happen in the first place. If it's foggy out, that's the trigger to remind the guys to be careful driving. Be diligent in training and making sure inventory systems are being followed so we aren't caught on a job without what we need.

Back to Ellen's restaurant example. Is there enough parking? Maybe there's trash in the parking lot. Whose job is that? Is that task in the daily procedures? Now we are walking up to the building. Is the front door smudged? Is the hostess at her station? How is the decor? How is the dress code? How do the scripts sound? Is the kitchen ready? This reminds me of "Kitchen Nightmares." What a phenomenal show for business owners to watch! Might not make a bad staff meeting either.

Maybe the first impression for your business is your Website or brochure. Maybe they call you on the phone. Do you have a procedure to make sure the phone is answered? Do you have a script and a system where that person has been empowered to deliver the most outstanding service experience?

Dressing for Phenomenal Success

I mentioned earlier that people make eleven important assumptions about you when they first meet you—and that happens within the first 30 seconds (before you even open your mouth).

The assumptions are:

1. Trustworthiness

2. Economic Level

3. Educational Level

4. Social Position

5. Level of Sophistication

6. Economic Heritage

7. Social Heritage

8. Educational Heritage

9. Success

10. Moral Character

11. Future Potential

Your Phenomenal Service Experience is going to be carried out by front-line team members who will either score high or low on these eleven points, so make sure you and your team are dressed and groomed well and that you have step-by-step service systems in place so that you don't have to reinvent the wheel each day.

Chapter 8

Phenomenal Administration Systems

Administration is tracking your numbers, the internal processes for running your office, and making sure you have adequate insurance and legal protection. *Phenomenal* administration is having an abundance of data you need to make the best decisions in your business when you need it. Phenomenal administration *systems* produce the data automatically and consistently.

Let's go back to your journey. The one and *only* reason your business exists is to be a *vehicle* to help you achieve your LIFE Goals. Your destination is living in freedom every day. Understanding that you are in exactly the place you are supposed to be. You are doing what you are called to do.

If you're on a journey, don't you need to know how you are tracking? You need mile markers. The GPS on an airplane tracks the miles flown and gives a chart that shows the route taken. Some commercial aircraft display the flight path and progress on the personal entertainment system on the back of the seats or on the overhead display screens. It shows passengers the route, and along the way they can see how much time remains until landing. Regardless of the type of vehicle you have, you need an instrument panel. Do we have enough fuel to get to our destination? What's our altitude? What's our attitude? How much longer do we have to reach our next goal? Can you see that without stats, you're actually driving *blind?*

The Guessing Gauge

When I graduated high school I was a long-haired rebellious teenager. It was a miracle that I actually graduated. The moment the ceremony was over, three of my friends and I jumped into my old car to drive to the beach to party for the weekend. I bought this jalopy for $250 with my paycheck from being a nighttime stocker at the grocery store. I had recently wrecked my good car, so my mama and stepfather took it away. I decided to show them that I didn't need them, and bought this jalopy when I wasn't even of legal age.

This car was so bad that the missing muffler caused an awful white smoke to billow up into the backseat of the car, which meant the windows had to be open, even if it was raining. Otherwise we would die! It probably won't come as a surprise that the gasoline gauge didn't work either. So I had to guess whether I had enough gas or not. And in those days we didn't fill up, we scraped up *change* when we needed gas! But here we were driving down one of those dark, lonely back roads of Alabama when we lost the "guessing gauge" game.

Two of us ended up walking for miles until a headlight appeared in the distance. As it got closer, we flagged down the car. The car was full of passengers, but they really wanted to help and suggested that we prop up the trunk lid and sit in the trunk. Before you know it, we're on our way down the road with our feet dangling out the back, watching the asphalt go by! They dropped some folks off and took us to get gas.

Most small business owners don't have enough data to make the right decisions and don't really know how to produce it. Most are using a "guessing gauge" in their business, rather than operating by real stats. If you are one of those who isn't paying attention to your stats, my bet is that you'll be shocked to find that the numbers aren't as good as you *think* they are. That's the bad news.

About ten years ago, I was asking one of my coaching members about his profit margin. "I don't want to know," he said. He went on to say that as long as he had money in his business account, he was okay. "Don't you want to know how you are really doing?" I pressed. "No, because I might get depressed!" he exclaimed.

The good news is that when you truly know how you are tracking on your life and business journey, you can make the course corrections you need to make. Having the right feedback is key to making a profit in your business and working smarter rather than harder. Remember that the *one and only reason* your business exists is to be a vehicle to help you achieve your life goals! If you look at the Wheel of Life, there is a financial spoke on that wheel. That spoke represents the amount of money you need to fulfill your life goals.

Now as Zig used to say, "Money isn't the most important thing in life, but it *is* reasonably close to oxygen!" He goes on to say, "Sometimes you really need it!" The fact is that your business must make a profit. If you want to have a phenomenally successful business that is profitable, predictable, and turnkey, you must address this area of your business. If you want to work less and make more, you've got to look at the finances of the business.

The point is, if you don't know what your stats are, you're driving blind! I never wanted to know anything about the numbers. I just wanted to take care of my clients. In fact, I didn't want to be a businessman. Imagine that? To me, a businessman was a boring, heartless person who only cared about money. Me? I just wanted to provide phenomenal customer service and I figured by doing that, my business would do well.

Do you realize that you can earn $2 million a year and spend $2.2 million? It's not hard! I hated the numbers. And for the longest time, I used what I call "The Elvis Presley Accounting Method." Have you heard of it? It goes like this: Elvis would buy a stranger a Mercedes and spend money like there was no tomorrow. As Priscilla and his step-father Vernon would get the bills back at Graceland, they were upset with Elvis. "How are we going to pay all these bills?" they demanded. "Don't worry about it, we can just get another gig!" was his response. And he could. He could just call his agent Colonel Tom Parker and do a million dollar deal on a tablecloth.

I lived that way for a long time. I know how to market. I know how to bring in the money. I once bought an entire fleet of trucks at one time. In those days, the banks and would give people all the credit they wanted if they had cash flow. I got into big-time debt. Eventually it became about paying all of the obligations. And that my friend, is *not* very phenomenal!

So I decided to understand the financials. I studied my financials until I just about went snow blind! I got a handle on my numbers. And that was good. But to get it systematized, I knew I needed a team. I realized that handling the administrative part of the business was not my gift. Yes, I still read my reports on a regular basis (just like you keep an eye on your instrument panel if you are flying an airplane), but you don't have to do it all yourself.

I hired financial consultants and built a system for that part of my business. I put a team in charge and put the accountability pieces in place so I know if anything is out of the ordinary. The people I have in that department love working with the numbers. I don't understand how that can be, but I am grateful for them because now our businesses are super profitable.

A business without a profit is just a hobby!

You may be like I was. You may love doing what you do. You may love serving your customers. You can be the best technical person in the world and be broke. You can be the best customer service person in the world and be broke. So if you're gonna go broke, why not enjoy it? Sit on your back porch and have a glass of tea. Go to the beach. Instead of working 24/7 going broke, have some fun! Has it occurred to you that those customers who don't want to pay your price aren't going to care that you can't retire?

Healthy Profits Cure All Other Business Evils

What are business evils? Taxes. Unpaid invoices that you have to write off. Employee pilferage. Damaged equipment or lost resources. Your former accountant didn't file your franchise tax properly and it cost you thirty-five grand. Sales didn't come in like you expected.

You've got to have healthy profits to overcome these things. You can no longer just squeak by. The recent recession caught a lot of business owners in a precarious position. They had not positioned themselves well and were getting by on thin margins to start with.

Healthy Profits Can Make a Worldwide Difference

When you have healthy profits, and no "evils" come along, guess what? You have extra money to do all sorts of wonderful things! Of course you can use it for your business to pay off equipment, to take your business to the next level, or you could bless your staff with bonuses. You can give money to your favorite charity or to someone who is struggling. I believe this is one of the biggest blessings of being a phenomenally successful business owner. I paid the rent on a church in Costa Rica for many years. I have been able to faithfully give to my church.

Not too long ago a friend's wife was deported to Columbia. She was 17 years of age when her parents brought her to the United States; they never got her paperwork properly completed. She is now 30 with two wonderful kids. What was she to do? She has no one in Columbia. It cost somewhere in the neighborhood of $25,000 to get her back legally. They didn't have that kind of money. But guess what? I and others were able to give thousands of dollars to bring her back. You cannot imagine the joy I felt to witness the reunion with her two children after being separated for eight months!

What difference can you make in the world with healthy profits? Maybe go on a mission trip. Support someone who is going. The need is endless in this world.

Tracking Your Numbers—as Easy as 1-2-3!

There's an old saying "Anything measured improves." It's funny how the human mind works. When you have actual data in front of you, and you have a written goal, it's interesting to see how just that process alone can improve the numbers.

Tracking and posting your numbers causes you to work hard on the strategies and systems to produce the result.

Here are the most important things to track: total sales, up-sells, sales by category, sales by source. Let's look at each.

Total Sales

Have you set your sales goal? If not, your tracking won't mean as much to you. And by the way, when you track your sales numbers, post them someplace you and your staff can see them every day. Even if you are a solo operator, post your sales goal and tracking where you see it several times a day.

Our subconscious minds are designed to go to work on problems even when we aren't thinking about them consciously. When you plant your sales goal in your mind several times a day, it gets burned into your subconscious. Humans do what humans see. Whatever controls your subconscious mind is going to turn into action (even when you aren't consciously thinking about it). This explains why setting a goal, writing it down and focusing on it every day works. You are working toward that goal without realizing it. This is a strange truth, but it does work, so be sure to post all of your goals and visions, not just your sales goal.

If you have daily transactions in your business, you want to track and post your sales *daily*. In high volume cases, you may even want to track sales by the hour. My oldest brother owns a McDonald's in Magee, Mississippi, and it is important for them to have an hourly pulse on the business because the labor decisions they make on an hourly basis determine whether they are profitable or not.

In my service company, we post our sales every day on a whiteboard so that our staff can see how we are doing. Each month we have a sales goal (which comes from our annual goal) and we post the daily sales and adjust our daily target based on the incoming data. This keeps the team focused on exactly what their goals are each day. Imagine you are on a long journey and you have determined that you need to travel a certain number of miles every day.

If you have a business that doesn't have daily transactions, then break it down in the smallest bites you can. For example, if you are in construction for example, it's project driven, so you want to track how many projects you've done in a certain amount of time and what your average projects are.

If your business is driven by membership or monthly continuity (like fitness training, business coaching, etc.), then you want to track the number of new memberships, retention, attrition, etc. It's all about the monthly billing.

If your business is driven by events, you want to track each event. For example if you are a professional speaker, what is your average fee, how much product did you sell at each event, etc.

The idea here is that before we can set our sales goal, we've got to track how we are doing.

Up-sells

As I shared in Phenomenal Sales Systems, the most profitable sale ever made is the up-sell, and this is definitely something you want to track. Again, track them as often as they happen and post them where everyone can see them.

Sales by Category

Every business should have multiple products or services (also called profit centers) so that you have more to offer the customer. This makes the up-sell possible and it gives you ways to grow. You need to know how much you are selling of each product and/or service.

For example, I have a member who is a tennis trainer in Australia. Most of her income is from tennis instruction for groups, but she has discovered she can make a lot of money selling tennis racquets, return nets, and even online training. And this is important because weather is a factor in her business since her group instruction is done outside.

Create a system where you can track each profit center individually. This can easily be done with industry-specific software, Infusionsoft or even on QuickBooks. When you look at these reports, you'll see the categories that are strong and those that aren't. Our natural inclination is to focus on the areas where there isn't much activity, but let me caution you that there may be a reason for that.

My friend Steve McKnight, who is Australia's number one real estate investment author, says, "Make sure there are hungry fish before spending too much time fishing." Instead, maximize your primary service and focus on the growing trends first. Then you can diversify into other areas. As you track those numbers, you can then begin to think about the various ways to sell more in each of your categories.

Sales by Source

Sales by source is tracking where your clients, patients, or members are coming from. Have they used your service before? Were they referred? Did they come from an advertising source? If so, which one and how much did it cost?

This is a very important area that is often overlooked. Even when it is tracked, it is usually done *incorrectly*.

The first step is to determine how much *repeat* business you have coming in each month. If your business thrives on repeat business, I hope you aren't making the "biggest marketing mistake of all," which is not marketing to past and existing clients. And if you are, I hope tracking these numbers will convince you that you need to take care of that.

This mistake warrants repeating…

I have often been coaching small business owners and they say, "I sent a mailer to my client base and didn't get a thing!" "Nothing?" I respond. "Nothing," they reply. "So you're telling me that you did not have one repeat customer the entire month?" I press. "Of course I did!" they retort. My next question is very soft and gentle, "Did you know that your clients are so busy that they may not have even remembered getting your mailer, but the very fact that you mailed something to them reminded them to call you?"

Sure you want to have a strong mailer with strong copy, but the fact is that people are busy and their minds are crowded with so much information, that when they get your mailer, they may not even read it. That does *not* mean that it didn't work. Because when they saw it, they planted in their minds, *I need to call them.* And one day for no apparent reason as they are driving down the road, it surfaced in their minds once again. And they took action. No, they didn't remember the offer. They may not have even remembered consciously getting the mailer.

But they *called!*

So how will you know if your client-based marketing is working? By tracking over a period of time. Client-based marketing should not be tracked the same way as advertising for new customers. Paid advertising for new customers is kind of like day trading. In day trading, you buy stocks that you want to give you an instant return. It's risky. Sometimes you win, sometimes you lose.

Client-based marketing is like a savings plan. You continue to invest a little bit every month and the value continues to grow. Over a long period of time it gets huge. I mentioned in Phenomenal Marketing Systems that the first time I realized this in my own business and increased my mailers from 4 to 12 per year, we saw a trackable increase of over $200,000. My cost was around $21,000. That was in 1999. Today that same business does almost $3 million per year and our repeat business is 65 percent of the total sales. Translation? Almost *$2 million a year* in *repeat* business! Can I afford to invest in marketing to past clients? I can't afford *not* to!

So, put a process in place to track *all* repeat business, not just the offer. Not just the campaign.

Step 2 is to track your *referrals*. How much business is coming in from referral sources? Who is referring you? How much did you do in referrals from your clients?

And finally, Step 3 is to track *new direct* business from paid advertising sources. For all paid advertising, you want to track the ROI dollar for dollar. For example, if you invest $1,000 and get $4,000 in new business from that source, you have a 4-to-1 return. When you understand your COGS (Cost of Goods Sold, explanation follows) and you begin to understand your "client acquisition" cost, you can make better decisions in your business.

Are you overwhelmed yet? Relax. Remember that once you learn this stuff, it will be an easy process. You will have phenomenal software that will spit this stuff out for you. In fact, as I was writing this section, I just popped over to my software to see how one of my campaigns was doing. I simply clicked on Orders for the date range and received instant feedback. When you are driving your car, how long does it take to see how much gas you have? Not long. Just a glance. That's because there is a system in place to report that to you.

And please answer this question for me: if you knew you could reach your ultimate life goals (your *ultimate* life goals), would it be worth figuring this out? If not, you won't do it.

Average Order

Whether you sell a product or a service, what is the average amount of each transaction? We have a coaching member in the remodeling business. If her income is $500,000 per year and she does 100 projects per year, her average order (project) is $5,000. What if she raised or lowered her prices? (See the following pricing section.)

Sales Closing Rates

Another valuable stat is tracking leads and prospect activity. Whether you have a traditional process where a prospect calls your company and you set up a sales presentation, or you have an online business where you are generating leads, you want to track this activity.

Perhaps you have prospects come to your store; you want to know how many customers came in and how many purchased. If you have a medical practice, how many clients came in and what did they buy? One of our coaching members is an optometrist. He gives the prescription for eye glasses or contacts, but that does not mean the patient will buy from his practice. It takes a specific strategy to make that happen consistently. With tracking, we know how many did and how many didn't. We can then begin to think about strategies to close more of those sales.

Now, let's go back to the remodeling company again. Let's say she does 200 proposals per year. If she did 100 projects, what was her closing rate? Fifty percent. If she increases the closing rate to 60 percent, the result would be 200 proposals x .60 = 120 projects x $5,000 = $600,000. That's $100,000 in additional revenue just by increasing the closing rate a little bit!

Average Production Rate

How much are you making per hour? How many man hours does it take to finish the project? How many products are you delivering per hour? If you can decrease the number of hours and keep the same revenue, you are making more per hour.

Returns or Re-Services

Returns and re-services are not only a financial cost, but also a branding cost. This is something that needs to be closely monitored. It's hard not to get emotional about refunds or returns. Instead, put your thinking cap on and find out how to solve the problem. Are you attracting the right type of client? Is it a service issue, or is it the way the product is being presented? If clients aren't doing their part, try to figure out how you can help them get more value.

Recently I got curious about my family tree and did the free trial on Ancestry.com. I found out some interesting things, but wasn't keen on keeping the subscription. That doesn't mean I don't think it's a valuable program. It just doesn't seem to be for me. Perhaps there are other services they could provide me with that I would want to subscribe to. But my guess is that the folks over at Anscestry.com aren't fretting over losing me as a customer. They have estimated how many people will stay with them and for how long. And they are *tracking* those stats to ensure they hit them.

Don't let your emotion drive your business decisions. For example, don't dump your guarantee because you have one or two people take advantage of it. Instead, how many people are you closing because you *have* the guarantee? How much more can you charge because you *have* the guarantee? How many more referrals are you getting because you *have* the guarantee?

Your Income Statement

Your Profit and Loss Statement (also known as your income statement) tells whether you made money or not. There are only five numbers on any income statement whether it's the smallest business in the world or one of Warren Buffet's companies.

My goal for you is for you to be able to plan your future income statement on the back of a business card. Once you understand these five numbers, you can create the picture simply and easily as you will see in just a moment, but you must understand each of the five numbers first.

1. **Income** - All the revenue or sales you make less refunds.

2. **COGS** - Cost of Goods Sold, also known as Variable Expenses are expenses that vary with the amount of income. This would

typically include labor and materials. I find that many small business owners are missing this vital stat. The goal here is to determine the running percentage of your COGS.

3. **Gross Profit** - Gross profit is the amount left over after subtracting the COGS from the total income. Also called the contribution margin as it is the amount that "contributes" to the overhead and profit.

4. **Fixed Expense** (also called overhead) - These are your expenses that don't change drastically with swings in revenue. Sure your advertising might change some, and you may have some things in fixed expense that vary depending on where your accountant has things listed on your Chart of Accounts, but basically it stays the same whether you do one dollar or a million in revenue.

5. **Net Profit/Loss** - This is the amount of money left over after all expenses. This is the amount that helps fund your life goals. Of course the amount listed here may or may not be the actual amount depending on depreciation, interest, and the way that accounting is done. However, when you create what I call a 12-month "cash flow budget," you can predict how much taxable income you will likely have once you know your first four numbers.

No matter how many line items you have on your income statement, they are grouped in five categories:

Income

- COGS (Cost of Goods Sold or Variable Expense)

=Gross Profit (or Contribution Margin)

- Fixed Expense (or Overhead)

=Net Profit/Loss

Creating Your Phenomenal Financial Future

The thing I love about being a business owner is that I can decide in advance how much money I want to make personally, and based on cost, figure out how much income my business needs to bring in for me to make that amount of money. Of course this all is "Lord willing." And I can do it with these simple five numbers. Let's take a look.

Start with the amount of cash you want to get from your business (remember you have to share a bunch of that with our greedy, inept government so they can borrow a bunch more money from China! UGH!).

So let's say you want to make $100,000. Now, we must figure out how much our fixed expense is. Let's say it is $50,000 for the year. That means our gross profit needs to be $150,000.

Here's the tricky part. We need to figure out what our COGS percent is to create our sales goal (total income). The way you do that is to track your labor and materials for as many periods as you can. Let's say that your COGS is 40 percent.

That means your gross profit will be 60 percent of the total income.

Now I can simply take my gross profit and divide it by .60, and that gives me my sales goal.

Here's the example:

$100,000 Net

$ 50,000 Fixed Expense

$150,000 Gross Profit

When I multiply the gross profit by .60, I get $250,000, which means I have to produce $250,000 in total income to make $100,000 net.

Here's the full picture:

$250,000 Income

- $100,000 COGS (40%)

=$150,000 GP (60%)

- $ 50,000 Fixed Expense

=$100,000 Net Profit

So now I know that I must figure out how to earn $250,000 in sales. That might mean I have to invest more in marketing or increase my overhead, which means I'll have to do more than $250,000. The idea here is to work backward. First figure out how much *you* need to make from that business. Then figure out the marketing strategies to bring that amount in and adjust the numbers as you plan those strategies.

Of course it never works out perfectly the first time, but anything measured improves; and as you get to know your stats and trends, you can plan your financial future much better. Zig Ziglar said, "Anything worth doing is worth doing poorly, until you learn how to do it well."

The phenomenal news is this: when you get this working, you can *continue* to increase your bottom line number! As you get good at building a business—growing sales and building a team—you can make as much money as you want! You just have to build the vehicle that will take you there.

Creating a 12-Month Budget

The previous was a simple sketch of the process. Now you want to create a 12-month budget. Forecast your income and expenses line by line for each month for the next 12 months. If you have QuickBooks, it's great to do it there because you can run a "Budget vs. Actual" report.

Caution: due to interest, depreciation, accounts receivable, the accounting method you use, and other factors, this will not translate into actual cash, so consider creating a 12-month *cash flow* budget. In this case, you will list the actual amounts you expect to come in and out during those times.

An income example is this. When we book a coaching client that will pay us over 24 months, we book in the entire amount as a sale in our CRM software, as the client has committed to the full amount. But we will budget the next 12 months' income for what we actually receive. An expense example is an equipment payment. If you have financed equipment, the interest and depreciation will show up on your income statement, but it will not match the actual payment. The tricky part of all of this is that you could be showing a profit and not have good cash flow. You can have great cash flow, but not be profitable. Eventually the cash flow runs out.

Accounts Payable

Be sure to always have a pulse on your monthly bills and be able to report your accounts payable at any point. You could be showing a lot of cash, but your outgoing bills can wipe it out quickly.

Accounts Receivable

This is who owes you. Another big mistake is not having a process in place to bill your clients and to follow up on a regular basis to make sure you get paid. In fact, don't bill people unless you absolutely have to. Ask for a credit application and/or take a company credit card that you will bill if you don't receive payment within 30 days. If you are servicing residential clients, it's insane to bill them unless they are ultra-wealthy and truly pay their bills with a check from the office.

A couple of years ago, I was conducting an on-site consultation for a contractor. He had about $400,000 in receivables in a business that was only doing about $800,000! I couldn't believe it. Upon investigating, I found that he wasn't sending the initial invoice until 90 days after the project. No *wonder* he had collection problems! He would get busy and didn't have a system to delegate this task to someone else.

At one of my conferences, I met with a couple on a break who had come to many of my meetings. I had become friendly with them, and they often opened up to me. The wife began to share how she was considering divorce because their business was struggling, and she felt it was his fault. She had always been responsible with her money and to go down with this ship was unacceptable to her.

While consulting with them, I found that their biggest problem was not sales, but cash flow. They weren't collecting their money soon enough. The bottleneck was due to the project manager not completing and filing the final paperwork at the end of the project (the husband was in charge of that department).

I asked them this question, "If you were collecting all of your money on time, would you have any financial issues in the company?" "No, we would be just fine," they both agreed. So I set up a simple system that made it easier for them to complete and submit the file to the client. And the best part was the husband had to physically take each and every completed file to the wife's office (she did the books), and she had to give him a kiss every time! No file, no kiss. It was a cute and fun little solution—and it worked. At this writing, they are smiling and still happily married.

Isn't it funny how one single thing can affect the entire business and even our lives? Especially when it has to do with money. Most divorces are triggered by money issues. The root cause is selfishness and irresponsibility, but the subject that gets the emotions going is usually financial.

Balance Sheet

Your balance sheet shows what you "own" and what you "owe." It tells the story of where you are and where you've been. It also reveals what your vehicle is actually worth. Your net worth is very important and it is increased by your *profit*. Although this is not something you'll stress over weekly or monthly, you do need to become familiar with it and follow it over time to make sure it is accurate and that you are increasing the net worth of the business.

The Only Three Ways to Increase Profits

1. Lower Overhead

If you have a large business with lots of fat, this may be an option for you. At one of my recent workshops, I was having lunch with the attendees. One was a guy who does business turnarounds. As he pulled into the parking lot of this $10 million company, it was filled with brand-new company vehicles. He knew immediately one of the reasons the company wasn't making a profit. Of course overspending is a symptom of a deeper root issue.

I like having new equipment, but not at the expense of going broke. If you are emotionally tied to stuff or people who aren't helping you become profitable, you need to get serious about what happens to all of those people and all that stuff if you keep losing money.

If you are a smaller business, you may actually need to increase your expenses. One of the things I routinely see in small business surveys, is that small business owners don't invest in enough marketing.

2. Lower Variable Costs

If you have production staff, materials, or product cost, this is the next area you can take a look at. Are you watching these areas? Are you being as efficient as you can be? If not, you may want to add Phenomenal Leadership Systems (next chapter) to your list.

3. Increase Sales

This is my favorite way to increase profits. I opened the chapter on Phenomenal Marketing Systems with the only three ways to increase sales: 1) increase sales from existing clients (by up-selling and marketing to your client base), 2) increase the number of clients you get, and 3) increase price.

This is a perfect time to talk about your price. If I didn't convince you that you could do it through marketing, perhaps I can convince you here.

How to Price Your Service for *Maximum* Profit!

Once you have your reporting sorted out, you can then begin to see what happens if you raise or lower your price. Remember that your goal is to make a maximum amount of profit, so you can have enough time left over for family, friends, and faith. You want freedom, and being profitable gives you the freedom to have options.

You may feel that your pricing is set by the market or by your customers. You may feel that it is set by what your competitors do. When you understand how to *differentiate* your business from others, and you finally understand that all of business is about relationships, and you begin to practice the proven principles of positioning yourself as the most desirable choice in your space, you can command higher prices.

The biggest consideration in pricing your services is your *cost* of doing business. Everything else is secondary. If you don't charge enough, you don't make the amount of profit you need to reach your life goals. Can you see how everything points back to that? The bottom line of your business funds your purpose in life. That's why your business exists. So to price your service for maximum profit, you've got to understand your cost. Here's a simple formula to figure this out:

Step 1: Determine Your Average Order (see previous). Let's say it's $250.

Step 2: Determine How Many Orders. Let's say in a one-year period you had 1,000 orders (or jobs, patient visits, coaching sessions, etc.) 1,000 orders at $250 = $250,000 for the year

Step 3: Determine Your COGS (Variable Expense) Percentage. Let's say it's 40 percent. $250 x .40 = $100 Gross Profit on each order

Step 4: Determine Your Fixed Expense (Overhead). Let's say it's $50,000

So, here's your picture again:

$250,000 Income

- $100,000 COGS (40%)

=$150,000 GP (60%)

- $ 50,000 Fixed Expense

=$100,000 Net Profit

Now simply do these two exercises with Price and Volume. Price is your average order. Volume is the number of units.

Scenario One

Raise Price, Volume Stays the Same. Let's say you raise your price 10 percent and don't lose any sales volume.

$250 x .10 = $275 per order x 1,000 orders = $275,000 for the year.

Now, here's your picture:

$275,000 Income

- $100,000 COGS (36%) (Amount stayed the same, but percentage went down!)

=$175,000 Gross Profit (64%) (Amount and percentage went up!)

- $ 50,000 Fixed Expense

=$125,000 Net Profit (The increase went straight to *profit!*)

Is it possible not to lose any customers when you raise your price? You bet it is. In fact, you may gain more clients! I've seen cases where the price was so low that prospects didn't believe the value was there.

Scenario Two

Raise Price and Lose Sales Volume. How much sales volume could you lose? Let's say you raise your price 10 percent, but you lose 10 percent of your sales volume.

$275 x 900 orders = $247,500

$247,500 Income (Income down only $2,500 but we are doing 10 percent less work!)

<u>- $90,000</u> COGS (36.3%)

=$157,500 GP (63.7%)

<u>- $ 50,000</u> Fixed Expense

=$107,500 Net Profit

You made $7,500 more by working less!

You can do these calculations many different ways to see how much sales volume you would have to lose for it to affect profit.

Special note: Don't get boxed into thinking you have to raise prices across the board. There may be certain products or services you need to lower your price on. You could raise your price only on certain items. For example, I had a client whose business was high-quality cleaning of expensive Oriental rugs, stone floors, and high-end carpets. One of the most time consuming parts of cleaning fine carpets in someone's home was cleaning the stairs. One year the only thing he raised his price on was stairs. The result—he made a *lot* more money!

Operations Tracking

Tracking is not exclusive to the financial side of the business. Marketing, sales, and expenses obviously have a direct impact on the numbers that can clearly be seen, but marketing and sales are supported and validated by service, which impacts the numbers in repeat and referral business.

The desired outcome of your Phenomenal Operations System is to exceed your clients' expectations—to wow them, to make them feel special. So how do you track that? Feedback from clients is the best way. Do you have a way of seeing what they see?

There may be many production stats to measure in your business (like production rates per hour as mentioned before), but here's a quick list of things to track that will help you in your small business if you aren't already doing them.

Client Feedback Surveys

As discussed in the Phenomenal Operations Systems chapter, 90 percent of unsatisfied customers will never let you know because they don't want to create a conflict. They have been trained that few business owners care enough or really know how to handle a complaint; it is easier for them to just go somewhere else.

Having a way for them to give you feedback anonymously is vital. A simple way to accomplish this is a survey. It can be online or offline and that depends on what they are buying and how it is delivered. In my service company, we include a simple 60 second survey in our Thank You Letter Package that they can mail, fax, or submit online. They do not have to include their name, so they can avoid the fear of retaliation.

We offer them the opportunity to insert their name and a testimonial. We also ask for a signature for permission to use the testimonial. Fortunately, most of the feedback forms we get are positive, but every now and then there is some kind of communication break down and there is something they are disappointed with—we respond immediately. In our seminars and conferences, we often hand out feedback forms. These forms help us see what resonates with the audience and what doesn't.

If you aren't getting enough feedback, give a gift for feedback. This is valuable information, so give them something for it. Many retail establishments and restaurants have a Website link on their receipt, but if there isn't something compelling to make me take time out of my busy schedule to do it, I won't. It might be better to have a way of doing it on check out.

On-Time Tracking

How often are your staff members on time to work? How often do you deliver your product or service on time? If you aren't on time, you've already blown the most phenomenal service experience. Having automatic reporting on these items can alert you to issues before they become epidemic.

Did you notice this section is titled "On-Time" Tracking not "Late" Tracking? The reason is that you want to recognize the good that people are doing; individual recognition is the most powerful motivator for humans.

Imagine a clean, white piece of paper with a black dot in the middle of the page. What do you see? A black dot! What does your employee see? All the white space on the page that represents what they did right. The black dot represents what they did wrong. Okay, okay, I know there is probably more than one black dot on the page, but when you become a phenomenal leader and you install a Phenomenal Leadership System, you will understand how to positively influence your team.

"I Caught You" Cards

These are cards on which team members or clients can recognize a team member for something specific. A fun thing to do in your team meetings is to read these and recognize those who are "written up" in a good way. I have noticed these cards at hotels as well. Track the number of positive comment cards received on specific employees and reward them for it. Behavior rewarded is behavior repeated.

Tracking Leadership Results

John Maxwell says, "Everything rises and falls on leadership." Everything that you have tracked so far is a result of leadership in one way or another. John also says, "The toughest person to lead is yourself," so even the results you are personally responsible for rise and fall on leadership.

Chapter 9

Phenomenal Leadership Systems

Leadership is *effectively* communicating your *vision, mission, and purpose.* *Phenomenal* Leadership creates a meaningful community where the vision, mission, and purpose is lived out. A Phenomenal Leadership *System* is a group of working parts that duplicates results consistently.

One of the biggest reasons small business owners remain prisoners of their own making is the lack of leadership skill. The owners of the business are convinced that no one is as capable as they are and are convinced they can't find "good" people.

I know how they feel. I have endured just about every employee nightmare you can imagine. I've had employees steal money from me, take my clients, and fail to show up for work leaving me to do the work all alone. And I know what it's like to feel like you can't find good people...

One sunny afternoon some years ago, my staff and I noticed a low-rider, gangster type vehicle sitting in our parking lot for quite a while. The two front doors were swung open and pot smoke billowed out of the car. There were two men in the car and about the time I was going to call the police, one of them got out of the car and began to make his way to our front door.

I was standing next to the phone in case I needed to call 911. *Is he going to rob us?* I wondered. *What could he possibly want from us?* He was wearing flip flops, cut-off blue jeans, a yellow tank top, and had a big tattoo on his arm. He didn't bother to take off his sunglasses as he stepped inside.

"Ya'll hirin'?" he asked.

You're kidding! I'm thinking to myself. I replied with something that is not exactly legal but seemed appropriate at the time. "We *do* require a drug test, is that going to be a problem?"

"Dat gon' be today?" he asked. In other words…if you give me 24 hours, maybe I'll pass it!

So I know it can be tough out there for employers to find employees. But I learned how to attract the best people, how to lead them, and most importantly have created a phenomenal leadership system that helps me attract, acquire, and train the very best people.

And you can too. You don't have to be held hostage by underperforming employees, bad attitudes, and downright insubordination. But in order to turn that around, you've got to become an effective leader. You've got to develop your leadership skill. The good news is that anyone can become an effective leader. It's a skill. And the better news, I mean *phenomenal* news is that you can develop a phenomenal leadership system. Your employees can be your greatest asset or your biggest nightmare. And that depends completely and solely on your leadership skill.

The first thing you must learn about leadership is that your team is your greatest asset. If you look at them as an expense, as a problem, or a "necessary evil," you're already off the rails. John Maxwell says, "Leadership is influence. Nothing more, nothing less. Everyone has influence in someone else's life." How do you gain influence? You "add value to people," John says. When you don't add value to them, you de-value them.

The biggest roadblock to getting cooperation from your employees is how *you* value them. This is the root issue. When you really *care,* you will treat them with the utmost respect and dignity. Dale Carnegie says that the number one thing that employees want is "sincere and honest appreciation." Every study that has been done has revealed that humans crave recognition and belonging far above how much their paycheck is every time. They aren't really aware of this, but it's true. (Now you have a little insider secret that they don't even know!)

When we *value* someone at the highest possible level, we will learn to communicate effectively with them. Zig says, "Encouragement is the fuel that people run on."

You may be thinking, *But Howard, my employees seem to always be messing up. How can I encourage that?* You don't encourage the *behavior,* you encourage the *person* so that you can help change his or her behavior.

Your team is your *greatest asset.* If you don't treat your team well, they won't treat your customers well in the long run. Sure you might get away with dictatorship for a while, but when the dictator isn't present, the followers don't care about the mission.

How do you turn this around? You first value them for who they are (and whose they are I might add—they're *not* yours!) Every human being is God's creation. We need to treat them that way. Don't worry, you won't have to let them get away with murder. We'll talk about how to get them to do what you want them to do in a minute.

But first, I want to talk about you and your ego. Part of our problem as business owners is we think we are all-important. And because I'm the boss, everyone else needs to bow down and do what I say. Sure, you're the boss and you should be respected. But you want to have the right kind of respect. Instead of forced respect, you want earned respect. There's a difference.

If you are willing to humble yourself, let your staff know that you care about them, and you want to make improvements that will benefit all, and you begin to become a better leader by learning and practicing proven leadership skills, and you press on to build a *phenomenal* leadership *system,* you will have a different business and life. I can promise you that.

One of the most rewarding parts of my life is watching my team grow professionally and personally. I have a little plaque in my private study that says "Success is making a difference in the lives of others. Happiness is watching them grow because of it." One of my core beliefs is that we are on this earth to love God and to love others—to make a difference. I think deep down everyone wants to make a difference. Do you?

No Team. No Dream.

Dave Anderson said, "If you have a dream, but no team, you've got to give up the dream or build up the team." Do you have a dream? Is your dream inspiring enough to create the desire you need to build a team? Remember, the *one* and *only* reason your business exists is to be a vehicle to help you achieve your life goals (your dream). You will not reach your biggest dreams in life by yourself. There are many things required to build a business that are simply out of your gift zone.

You can't do everything yourself. There isn't enough time in a day to successfully implement all 12 functions on your organizational chart by yourself. Can you outsource a lot of what you do? Sure, but that still requires leadership. How do you handle it when your vendor or virtual assistant doesn't come through for you? Don't you need influence with everyone you work with, other than threatening to fire them?

Discovering how to lead and build a team set me free to do the things I love to do. I have a staff of 40 who run my companies for me, and I can travel the world without having to be involved in every detail. I learned what leadership is. I developed myself as a leader. I then began developing my people to be leaders. Then I applied my systems approach to leadership just like the other areas of my businesses. The result? I can travel the world, take as much time off as I want, and live my dream—because I built a team. That is the reward.

I have also found that developing people is the most gratifying things you can do in life. It thrills me to see my people grow as leaders. Today I have a phenomenal staff that wants to win. They *want* to do it right. How have we turned it around? *Phenomenal* Leadership *Systems*. First, I had to learn how to be an effective leader. Next, I had to build a phenomenal leadership *system* that would help my team win consistently and that would continue to develop them.

I believe anyone can learn how to be a more effective leader, which will help you attract and develop the right people. And when you do that, you will be on your way to reaching your biggest dreams in life. Remember, you must give up the dream or build up the team. You won't reach your biggest dreams in life by yourself. You will remain in the prison cell called your small business doing everything yourself.

Definitions of Leadership

Dale Carnegie said, "Leadership is enlisting the willing cooperation of others to achieve a goal." First, you've got to have a goal. You must have a vision. You must know where you are going. And notice he said the "willing" cooperation of others.

Former President Dwight Eisenhower said, "Leadership is the art of getting someone else to do something you want done because *he* wants to do it." How do you do that? By adding value. They want to please you. As a leader, you must create desire by sharing a vision.

Zig Ziglar's famous quote was, "You can have everything in life you want if you just help enough other people get what they want." This usually isn't identified as a leadership quote, but I would put it at the top of the list. Think about what you want. What do others want? You can have everything in life you want if you just help enough other people get what they want. If you aren't getting everything you want, maybe you need to help some more people!

Is there more you can do to add value to your staff? The answer is yes. We are never done giving. We are never done developing. We are never done building others up. Ever. The first time I interviewed Zig Ziglar, I told him that he stole his quote from Jesus. Jesus said, "Give, and it will be given back to you, pressed down, shaken together and running over." Zig just laughed and said, "Well, I know Him personally, so I'm sure that's okay!"

I had the pleasure of going to Microsoft with John Maxwell and one of his high-level groups. He had Kevin Turner, the Chief Operations Officer (COO) talk to us about leadership. Kevin said, "Leaders are coaches. The original definition of coach was to bring a person from where they are to where they want to be." Think of the old stage *coach* in the Wild West. The stage coach would bring people from one point to another.

Here are some points I took from Kevin's talk:

- A coach gets you from where you *are* to where you need to *be*.

- A coach *inspires* you to reach your peak potential.

- A coach holds you *accountable*.

- A coach ensures you have received *training*.

- A coach makes sure you are in the right *position*.

- A coach exercises *authority* while remaining *responsible*.

A Leader is NOT...

A leader is not God!

Many years ago I felt like I was carrying my team. I poured out my leadership woes on my mentor. After patiently listening to my problems, he responds by saying, "Howard, I'm afraid you're suffering from the fear of rejection!"

"What?!" No way. Not me. I am one of the most confident people I know. But the more I thought about it, I knew it was true. I would let people run over me because I wanted to avoid conflict.

This was revelation to me. It was very freeing to know that I didn't have to make everybody happy. I didn't have to make sure everyone was content. In fact, I realized at that moment that I was hurting myself, my company, and especially my employees.

My mentor went on to show me that by trying to be the "provider" of their emotional health and carrying the burden of their financial well-being, I was actually playing God and that was a huge sin! *Oh great. Not only am I miserable, but I'm sinning too? This is not good.* I could reject everything he was saying, but I knew it was true. When I started looking at all my relationships, I noticed that I avoided conflict at all costs—and carried the burden for it.

This was happening in my marriage too. When my wife and I disagreed, she would fight tooth and nail, and I would withdraw. Psychologists call this *fight or flight*. There are many hidden emotions at work here. We are conditioned to deal with conflict by the environment we grew up in and our own value systems. To add fuel to the fire is our preferred communication style. I learned that when my wife's family raised their voices or argued, it didn't mean they were really angry and upset. It didn't mean they hated each other. I learned that when Italians shout and argue, it's just how they communicate. So I found that I could get along with my wife better by fighting back a little bit! And then I got even smarter; now I crack a joke and make light of the situation (as long as it isn't too serious).

For me, withdrawal was normal. This is how my family communicates. We don't want to offend. We would rather go away and think about the situation, and come back for another discussion. If my wife withdraws, it means she is super offended. When she goes quiet, I better get in the car, get out of the house, and come back with flowers!

Most human beings have not really learned how to deal with conflict properly, and how to truly level with people. They haven't learned how to be totally transparent and honest. They don't know how to be real during conflict. There are many fears underneath. This affects us greatly as leaders. If you can't be open and direct because of deep-seated fears of your own, you'll struggle as a leader.

A leader is not the only one who thinks.

The Dale Carnegie Institute's Leadership Training for Managers states, "People support a world they help create." It can feel lonely as a business owner, especially if you have challenging decisions to be made. I have found that it helps tremendously to get my team together and let them think about the problem, decision, or opportunity. In fact, some of our best ideas and solutions didn't come from me. They came from the team. Your dream team consists not only of your staff, but your mentors, coaches, and consultants as well.

A leader is not the only leader.

Everyone in your organization influences someone and is therefore already a leader. The questions are: What kind of leader are they? And how are they influencing others? Developing leaders instead of just followers is key to long-term success. Are you teaching your staff how to be phenomenal leaders? As you learn it, pass it on to them.

A leader is not the only important one.

Yes, we know you're the boss. Everybody knows, so now, get over the ego, wake up and smell the leadership coffee and get with the program. When you get over your self-glorifying agenda and realize that your employees are your greatest asset and that your team is what will help you reach your dream, you'll begin to treat them differently.

A leader is not a manager.

There is a tremendous difference between a leader and a manager. A good manager supervises production and protects assets. A leader develops people. A phenomenal leader doesn't have to be the best manager, but everyone including the manager must be a leader for phenomenal success.

A *Phenomenal* Leader IS...

One who loves God.

In his book *Spiritual Leadership,* Henry Blackaby says, "Leaders who know God and lead in a Christian manner will be phenomenally more effective in their world than the most skilled and qualified leaders who lead without God."

One who loves others.

Everyone wants to be loved. Everyone wants to be accepted and understood. When you show people how much you value them as human beings, you will see an amazing return of loyalty and care from your team. I tell my staff as well as my members how much I love them all the time. Why? Because I do! I really do care about them. I agree with this well-known saying, "No one cares how much you *know* until they know how much you *care*."

One who is a positive role model.

Being a leader is a big responsibility. It shouldn't be taken lightly, but it shouldn't be avoided either. The rewards of making a difference in others' lives is astounding. As I mentioned previously, I have a little plaque in my home study that says "Success is making a difference in the lives of others. Happiness is watching them grow because of it." Doesn't it make you happy when you help someone with their life? If you can't get inspired by that, I don't know what you can get inspired about.

One who is inspired.

Speaking of inspiration, our slogan in my membership program is "Inspiration to Implementation." Have you noticed that the most successful business owners are those who are excited about the future? Are they inspired because they are growing? No, they are growing because they are inspired!

What are they inspired about? They have vision. In his last book, *Born to Win,* Zig Ziglar wrote, "The most important ingredient for success is desire and desire comes from vision." Where does vision come from? Inspiration. Where does inspiration come from? Books like this one. Stories of people doing what you want to do. When I was a 23-year-old waiter making just enough money to pay the rent on my apartment, I went to New Jersey to get married. A friend of the family who was my same age was tooling around in a little red Mercedes convertible. The desire that came from that vision was the result of getting excited about the possibilities of having that kind of lifestyle for myself.

One who is hopeful.

A leader is a dealer in hope. If we don't have hope for the future, why do anything? This is the unfortunate condition of average, non-thinking people today. They have no hope because they are listening to the news and listening to other people who are uninformed in human potential, the grace of God, and the possibilities that entrepreneurs can discover. We must not only have hope, but deal hope. We must not only have hope, but demonstrate hope. We must not only have hope ourselves, but we must show evidence of hope by sharing success stories.

One who is enthusiastic.

Before I got healthy, I had frequent migraine headaches. They were awful. My entire body hurt. Literally from the top of my head to the tip of my toes. Sometimes they were so bad I was actually sick. On a trip to Amsterdam, my wife and I were touring some beautiful gardens and I was having an episode. After observing me keeled over throwing up, a young Dutchman offered to help us find a doctor.

We followed him in the rental car to a nearby doctor's office (which was an adventure on its own—sharing a round-about with a million bicycles, pedestrians, trolley cars, buses, other cars and taxi cabs driving on the rail-road tracks to get around everyone else). After waving us off, I entered the doctor's office only to find that it was a veterinarian clinic! And the amazing thing about socialized medicine was that he was able to write a prescription for me!

Even though I was hurting, I had to be enthusiastic in front of my staff. As soon as you allow yourself to focus on your problems, you give everyone else the same permission. You are the example. My staff meetings were always upbeat and positive. No matter how I felt, I had to be enthusiastic for my team. This doesn't mean you don't have real feelings and that you never share them. It just means that we have to make sure we are sending the right message.

Fortunately, about eight years ago I got healthy, and the migraines went away for good. This is how dumb I was. I didn't eat breakfast. I drank breakfast. Lots of strong coffee. I didn't eat lunch until two in the afternoon. The excuse was "I'm busy!" When I got home at the end of the day, I was famished. I ate everything in sight. Step one was to eat a bunch of Doritos (nacho cheese flavored), then a pile of barbequed pork chops with a heap of my smashed potatoes seasoned with butter, green onions, and bacon bits. After some TV, back for seconds and then French vanilla ice cream, topped with bananas and Hershey's chocolate syrup! But I'm not done yet. Late night TV required some tortilla chips and my favorite salsa. And I wondered why I had migraines? How unaware can a person be!

So no matter how you feel, no matter who did what to you, or what circumstances you face, you'll do better as a leader to be enthusiastic in front of your team. I don't recall if it was Dale Carnegie or one of the many networking groups I attended, we were asked to stand up and say, "Act enthusiastic to be enthusiastic!" as we clapped our hands together. Maybe it was NLP, who knows. But it works.

To quote my hero once more: Zig said, "You can't do anything with a positive attitude, but you can do everything better with a positive attitude than you can with a negative one." Research reveals that being enthusiastic and having a positive attitude actually changes the vibrations of your brain and actually has an affect on how you feel.

One who is growing.

Anything not growing is dying. Leaders are readers and learning makes you grow. Continuing to learn keeps your mind sharp and helps you with new ideas. The fact that you are this far in this book tells me you are interested in growing. Continue to develop yourself and transfer what you learn to your team.

One who is seasoned.

My mama in Alabama works at a retail store. She used to be the manager, but gave that up to enjoy her life a bit more. Why in the world she still works at 76 years of age is beyond me, but that's another story. She's just like that. She wants to stay busy and likes the interaction. The manager is now a young man and she tells me how he underestimates how long things will take. Inventory for example. She has the experience and knows the reality of how long things will take. As he gains experience, he'll get more realistic. Treasure experience as a leader.

Phenomenal Leaders are Phenomenal Communicators

My definition of leadership is *effectively communicating* your **vision, mission, and purpose.** Let's go back to GPS for a moment. Your vision is *where* you are going, your mission is *how* you will get there, and your purpose is *why* you do what you do. The key to phenomenal leadership is effective communication. John Maxwell wrote a book called *Everyone Communicates, Few Connect*. When I say "effectively" communicating, I mean connecting. I mean that people are following. You can *tell* your staff what the vision, mission, and purpose is, but unless they are actually doing it, you haven't gotten through yet.

Wikipedia states that the word *communicate* comes from the Latin word *communis*, meaning "to share." I find this interesting because my belief (and experience) is that humans have a deep longing for belonging. We want to be part of a community that has a sense of shared vision, mission, and purpose.

Long before I looked up the word "communicate" on Wikipedia, I shared my definition of leadership; so I was surprised and delighted to see the following excerpt from Wikipedia:

Barriers to effective human communication

Physical barriers

Physical barriers are often due to the nature of the environment. An example of this is the natural barrier which exists if staff are located in different buildings or on different sites. Likewise, poor or outdated equipment, particularly the failure of management to introduce new technology, may also cause problems. Staff shortages are another factor which frequently causes communication difficulties for an organization. Whilst distractions like background noise, poor lighting or an environment which is too hot or cold can all affect people's morale and concentration, which in turn interfere with effective communication.

System design

System design faults refer to problems with the structures or systems in place in an organization. Examples might include an organizational structure which is unclear and therefore makes it confusing to know who to communicate with. Other examples could be inefficient or inappropriate information systems, a lack of supervision or training, and a lack of clarity in roles and responsibilities which can lead to staff being uncertain about what is expected of them.

Attitudinal barriers

Attitudinal barriers come about as a result of problems with staff in an organization. These may be brought about, for example, by such factors as poor management, lack of consultation with employees, personality conflicts which can result in people delaying or refusing to communicate, the personal attitudes of individual employees which may be due to lack of motivation or dissatisfaction at work, brought about by insufficient training to enable them to carry out particular tasks, or just resistance to change due to entrenched attitudes and ideas.

Ambiguity of words/phrases

Words sounding the same but having different meaning can convey a different meaning altogether. Hence the communicator must ensure that the receiver receives the same meaning. It is better if such words are avoided by using alternatives whenever possible.

Individual linguistic ability

The use of jargon, difficult or inappropriate words in communication can prevent the recipients from understanding the message. Poorly explained or misunderstood messages can also result in confusion.

However, research in communication has shown that confusion can lend legitimacy to research when persuasion fails.

Physiological barriers

These may result from individuals' personal discomfort, caused—for example—by ill health, poor eyesight or hearing difficulties.

Presentation of information

Presentation of information is important to aid understanding. Simply put, the communicator must consider the audience before making the presentation itself and in cases where it is not possible the presenter can at least try to simplify his/her vocabulary so that the majority can understand.

Wow! How many of these communication mistakes are small business owners making? "Simply put, the communicator must consider the audience…." What if we really understood people? How much more effectively could we communicate with them? What if we truly understood human behavior? What if we understood the needs, wants, and desires of others? When I started my business I didn't want to know about human behavior. I just wanted to make my customers happy. But I learned that understanding human behavior is the key to marketing, sales, customer service, and leadership.

In order to communicate better, it is important to understand others. Each of us have a different way of communicating. Understanding these communication styles helps us to connect better. I am grateful for the various behavior assessment programs that are available as they have helped me understand myself and others so I can communicate more effectively.

There are a number of programs available, and we use an in-depth program in my training systems, but the DISC Profile is a simple tool that has been especially helpful to me over the years. I will share a bit about that later.

Vision, Mission, and Purpose

The vision is the destination. Let's say we're going on vacation (holiday). Where are we going exactly? Where are we going to stay? What will we do when we get there? You don't go on vacation without a clear vision of where you are going, right? When you buy an airline ticket, you have to tell the agent exactly what city you are going to, correct? When you get in a taxi, you tell the driver exactly where you are going.

"Vision + Vision = Division"

Dion Robert pastors a church of over 100,000 people on the Ivory Coast of Africa. He said, "vision + vision = division." If you and your team are pulling in different directions, eventually division comes. Many years ago I had two partners. All three of us had different gifts. I was the sales and marketing guy (and the president, the leader), one was the operations guy, and one was the administration guy. When we worked together it was a thing of beauty. Each was passionate about his area. Each was competent in his area.

The business grew by leaps and bounds. Eventually, three different visions emerged regarding where we should go with the business. After a couple of years of struggling with each other in disagreements about what should and shouldn't be done, one of the partners finally bowed out. I was happy to oblige him and paid him what he wanted. He still works for me today and is a phenomenal person. Just because people have different opinions doesn't mean they're wrong or are bad people. In fact, had we done some of the things he wanted to way back then, I would have avoided a great deal of heartache later on.

Once Scott was out of the picture, Dennis and I went after each other even more aggressively. I didn't realize poor Scott was the buffer between us two "bulls"! Dennis went on to be a trainer, which he loves to do, and both of them made out very well financially. I got my company back and was able to pursue my vision, which not only eventually led to a predictable, profitable turnkey operation, that business is the envy of its industry, and I am living my dream helping other business owners stop being slaves to their businesses.

There can be only one vision. We can't be on our way to Florida and Texas at the same time. We can go to one first and then go to the other. We can stop by one on the way to the other, but if I'm in Alabama, I can't be on my way to both at the same time.

Michael E. Gerber said in his book, *Awakening the Entrepreneur from Within,* "A vision is comprised of your primary aim and your strategic objective. The first is the vision for your life. The second is the vision for your business. Together, these two visions become the driving force for the growth of the company."

You see, *together* these become the driving force. Your business vision must reinforce your life goals. Otherwise you'll be conflicted. Be clear on both and communicate them to your staff.

Get Your Dream Team Involved in the Vision

Even though there can only be one vision, I would have done better by incorporating some of my partners' ideas into my vision. Over the years I got better at listening to others (as my friend Tom Ziglar says, "Your hearing gets much better after you've failed a few times."). Now I include my team in the vision casting. Dale Carnegie said, "People support a world they help create." Today, when I have a challenge or a problem or want to brainstorm, I get my team together. And I have to admit that some of our very best ideas didn't come from me.

Your Phenomenal Vision

Your Dream

Your dream is the inspiring picture that engages your mind, will, and emotion, empowering you do everything you can to achieve it. Get your team involved in the dream. The dream includes everything you want to *be, do, and have* as a company. People want to work for people who have dreams. People want to be associated with successful people. People want to work for a company that has dreams of being something special.

Your Values

Who are you as a group? Zig Ziglar said if you want to have something different, you've got to do something different. And to consistently do something different, you've got to be something different. The actions you take are directly related to *who* you *think* you are. As a leader, you must develop your team to understand who they are.

Who you are is defined by your *values*. What do we really value as a team? We can say we value the customer, but does it really show up in our actions? We can say we value one another, but does it really show up in our daily routine? We can say we value making a profit, but when there isn't any, we better do a values check to see what we value higher than profits.

We value what we do and we do what we value. There is no escaping this truth! I can say I value health, but if I don't exercise and eat right, I value something more than health! Look at how you *act* as a team and you will see what you value.

Your Culture

The end result is your values (what you do as a group). The most important thing in a company is its culture. The company culture is the sum total of who we are. It is the reality of our character as a team. It is *who* we really are. Your culture is defined by your values.

Each person who comes into your company has a different value set. Each person has a different way of handling conflict, celebrating success, and dealing with failures. Their values may or may not be constructive. As a company, you've got to adopt the values you want the company to live by and effectively communicate them to your staff.

I adopted these five *values* for my companies:

1. *Reputation* - We will protect and build our reputation by keeping our conduct above reproach.

2. *Experience* - We will gain every ounce of experience we can in our field so we can bring proven solutions to our clients.

3. *Education* - We will thoroughly train ourselves and stay on the cutting edge of education in our field so we can bring our clients the latest solutions.

4. *Systems* - We will build systems in our business so we can consistently provide the same level of service experience to our clients every time.

5. *Guarantee* - By honoring our guarantee, we reinforce our reputation.

Do these five values sound familiar? If you noticed that these are also the five points shared in our marketing, you are exactly right!

Doesn't it make sense to live by the same values you are offering? Doesn't it make sense to teach your staff members to live by these values so the client is going to consistently get what they are buying? On a CD I listened to once, a company called Y2 Marketing talked about the "outside perception" of a company and their "inside reality." The outside perception communicates who you are, and your inside reality is what really happens when people buy your product or service.

Many companies have a phenomenal outside perception, but fail to deliver. Others have a phenomenal inside reality, providing the most phenomenal service experience ever, but fail to market it properly. What if you had both? What if your people delivered on the promise every time? That's what living out our values is all about.

Your Goals

Do you have specific, measurable, achievable goals for your staff? Is your sales goal posted? Do you have production goals? Do you have profit goals? Part of your vision is your goals. Your goals are the points along the route that you want to reach in a specific time frame. I drive from my home in the Houston area to my place in Destin, Florida, on a regular basis.

The goal is my specific location in Destin. I know how much time it takes to get to each city. I know that when I've been driving two and one half hours, I should be in Lake Charles, Louisiana. I know when I get to Pensacola, Florida, I've got about an hour and a half to go. These time frames work out just fine as long as I don't run out of gas, there aren't any traffic jams, or I don't get distracted and turn onto a scenic route.

All of these have happened to me over the years. I have no idea why I admit the following, but one time my wife and son were in the car with me coming back from Destin. They were both asleep, and I was all worked up over a piece of property I wanted to buy. I was completely and utterly consumed in thoughts and imaginations, when the unthinkable happened. I let my brand-new Lexus run out of gas! How can that happen? That was my wife's question for sure!

I've been making that trek for many years, so many things have happened such as light posts have fallen, thunderstorms so heavy I couldn't see the lights in front of me (along with lightning so close I thought the glory of God had come down on me it was so bright), and many accidents. Fortunately I've never been in an accident on that stretch. One time a tanker truck exploded and the freeway was completely shut down. I got out my GPS and formulated a route through some small Louisiana towns. *Hours* later I was back on the freeway.

The point is that these kinds of things happen in your business. It won't always be smooth sailing. But if you don't have a goal, if you don't even know where you are going and when and if you ever get there, all you'll know is that you don't have gas, or there are problems. When you have clear-cut goals, you'll know how you are progressing on the journey.

Your Phenomenal Mission

One of my favorite quotes is this Japanese Proverb:

Vision without action is a daydream.

Action without vision is a nightmare.

You can have a phenomenal vision, but if you don't take action, it's just a daydream. This is where your phenomenal mission comes in. The mission is *how* you will get where you are going (GPS). The mission was covered in a previous chapter, but remember the mission is what your team *does* every day. Unfortunately, most small business owners live in the second part of this proverb. "Action without vision." When there is no vision and no mission, you are subject to whatever is happening in the news. And that, my friend, is a nightmare!

Be sure to go back to the chapter on building systems in your business and make sure you have established your phenomenal mission. The mission is the *strategy* to reach the vision. It's the one thing that we know if we accomplish it, the vision will come. They are connected. In fact, your mission guides your every decision. If your mission is to provide the most phenomenal service experience ever, you have to decide who wants that. Not everyone does. Some people just want a low price. That determines what kind of marketing you do. The mission determines what your dress code is, what kind of materials you have, and what the decor in your office is.

The mission establishes your *desired culture.* Your values shape your desired culture. Actually fulfilling the mission means you are living out those values that establishes your desired culture. When everyone is fulfilling the mission, the values are being lived out and the vision is being reached.

Let me say that as a leader, you've got to live out the mission yourself if you expect others to do the same. You must be so passionate about the mission that it practically oozes out of you. Are you *that* passionate about the mission? Or do you find yourself focusing more on the activities in front of you?

Whatever you focus on is what your team will focus on. They see what you do as most important. They see your true values being lived out. Or worse, if you aren't connecting with them at all, they'll focus on whatever's happening around the water cooler. As the leader, you must determine what the mission is, why it is important, and communicate it to your team.

A phenomenal mission adds value to your team because they get to go out and do something important. Most people who go to work don't have any passion for what they do. That is death to a company. Breathe life into your company by adding a phenomenal, passionate mission onto your inspiring, compelling vision.

Your Phenomenal Purpose

Immature leaders declare, "Don't ask me *why*, just *do* what I say!" Many of us have failed as leaders, not only in the workplace, but at home because we don't take the time to share the "why" behind the "what." If there's anything I've learned (the hard way) is that the why helps a staff member understand the importance of a task or duty. If they don't know *why*, it has no meaning.

Phenomenal leaders continually explain why. This is one of the most important lessons you can get from this chapter. If your folks don't know why they are doing what they do—if they don't know the purpose, it doesn't have meaning.

Your *purpose* is the *why* behind what you do. A few years ago I was sitting in the sun by the pool working on my goals as I often do. I was putting down some BIG dreams! As I looked at those big dreams, two questions came to me, *Why do I want all of that? Why do I want to do all of this?* And the answer came shortly after. I realized that I had a mission and calling to fulfill. The things I had on the list were either things to help me accomplish the mission, or they were rewards for accomplishing the mission.

Zig Ziglar said, "It's not what you get when you reach your goals, it's what you *become.*" Zig has a goal-setting process that starts with dreams, then you turn them into goals and ask that all important question, "Why?" after every goal. He goes on in the process to help you make sure that your goals are "fair to everyone involved." And can I tell you that if your goals don't make a difference in the lives of others, you'll have a bunch of stuff and be empty.

That may be a reason why you don't even try to reach your goals—you see a bunch of empty people with a lot of stuff. Sad.

But I'm here to tell you that if you have a purpose that you are passionate about, and you help enough other people get what they want, you'll get what *you* want! Why should we do anything without a good reason? Why should we do anything that isn't going to add value to others?

So be clear on your purpose. Be clear about your why. Make your WHY really big and really meaningful so that your folks can't wait to get to "work" so they can reach their goals by helping the company reach its vision, accomplish the mission, and live out the purpose. It's a thing of beauty when it works.

The DISC Profile

As I mentioned earlier, the DISC profiling system has been helpful to me. As I pen this section, I'm in Costa Rica with my wife, my 76-year-old mama from Alabama, my brother and his wife, along with two of my clients, Bruce and Joanna DeLoach.

Bruce and Joanna are technical trainers (who do a phenomenal job in their industry by the way), and we were talking about this process by the pool. Bruce couldn't stand it anymore. He had to know "what" he was. He took the DISC profile online and it explained why he was so much fun to be around.

The DISC Profile reveals four basic communication styles: *outgoing* and *reserved*, and *people*-oriented and *task*-oriented:

D = Dominant. This style is *outgoing* and *task*-oriented. The D style is direct and to the point. They are usually in a hurry and impatient, and they can be demanding. They can be good CEOs because they like to be in charge, and they know how to get things done. The weakness of the D is they are in such a hurry to get things done, they forget that people are around! They can be too hasty, which causes all sorts of problems.

I = Influential. This style is *outgoing* and *people*-oriented. They are the life of the party. They love people and they love to talk. Since they love people, they make good outside sales and marketing reps. Their weakness is they aren't detailed, so things can fall through the cracks.

S = Steady. This style is *reserved* and *people*-oriented. They are concerned about the welfare and feelings of others. Since they are reserved, they don't seek the limelight. Many times they have a servant attitude and make great customer service people. Their weakness is that they can get their feelings hurt easily.

C = Competent. This style is *reserved* and *task*-oriented. They are cautious and calculating. They are analytical and make great accountants. This is the person you want to read a contract or to crunch numbers. Their weakness is they can come off very critical and negative.

Do you know anyone who fits one of these communication styles? What about you? Of course you want to take an assessment to see how you score in each of the areas, but you probably see some of these characteristics in yourself and those you know well.

This is probably the briefest outline of DISC on the planet, but it gives you a quick overview of how people have different behavior and communication styles. As you learn more about this, you'll see that most everyone has a combination of the two letters and that their dominant style will show more or less in different situations.

Many times their style will show up differently when they are at work or at home, under stress or not. And please understand this is not to put a label on anyone. It is simply to understand how they communicate and what kind of environments they will prosper in.

Now, how will you use this information? When you understand your behavior style, and you understand the dominant behavior style of others, you can adapt to their style. Notice I said "adapt to *their* style," not force them to adapt to yours.

Suggestions for Communicating with the Four Styles

When communicating with Ds, get to the bottom line. Don't take too much of their time. Understand that the more of their time you take, the more restless they become. They may even look at their watch because the day is passing by and they're thinking about their "to-do" list. Do make sure you get important information across to them. You don't want to leave out something really important. Start with the bottom line and they'll ask you for the details as they want them.

If you are in a situation where you have to give them a lot of detail, or take them through a process (like the seven step sales system), prep them for it and let them know the benefit of being patient for a moment.

When communicating with Is, indulge in their stories. They love to talk about other people, events, and ideas. Let them talk! Smile and laugh with them. They will love you for it.

The S is all about people and feelings. Talk about family and friends and meaningful relationships. Tell them how much you appreciate them.

When communicating with Cs, go slowly and give the details. Be patient. They don't make decisions quickly, so give them time to process and analyze.

Scott, who runs my Administration Department is a high C. He is perfectly fit for that role, but my D is dominant, so I've learned over the years that I have to go slowly with him. I know he'll have a lot of questions. I am patient with the process. I know he won't make a quick decision like I do as a D. Most often that works to our favor because he sees things I miss as a D.

Help your team understand the various communication styles. It is very helpful for you to understand the different communication styles as it helps you communicate with your staff better, but it is extremely important for your staff to learn this so they can communicate with each other and with clients and vendors.

For example, when a high I and a high C have a conflict, get ready for some fireworks! The I is looking at the relationship, and the C is looking at the bottom line. Another example is how Ds can be in so much of a hurry they overlook the sensitivity of an S and hurt their feelings. It's really fascinating to watch, but if you aren't aware of these behavior and communication styles, you won't know why you aren't getting through to someone or why they are not getting along with one another.

In a sales situation, your team members need to speed up for the D, slow down for the C, be fun for the I, and sensitive for the S. It's remarkable to see this at work in a sales situation or dealing with a vendor.

How to Hold Phenomenal "Meetings"

I hate meetings. I'm not sure why, but meetings feel like one of those old vinyl records that all of sudden goes into slow motion. As an "off-the-charts D" I want everything moving and moving fast! But I have found that it's impossible to communicate effectively if you don't meet with your team on a regular basis.

Meetings give you an opportunity to share the vision, mission, and purpose as well as get feedback from your team. Most importantly, it's your opportunity to build community in your business. Having a positive, productive staff comes down to communication. Regular "meetings" are the way to make that happen.

I hesitate to use the term "meeting" because it has a negative connotation. You may want to adopt the term I learned from my friend, Kirby Lammers. Kirby always called his staff meetings a "family reunion." He goes on to say, "No negative energy allowed." The last thing you want to do is allow your meetings to turn into a gripe session. If you don't give your staff a positive, phenomenal vision, mission, and purpose, they will automatically focus on what's wrong. It's human nature. Make all of your meetings positive.

The Success Formula

Start *all* of your meetings with recognition and praise. You want to build a culture of praise. Dale Carnegie said the number one thing employees want is sincere and honest appreciation. You might start out with who's top in sales or read testimonials. Depending on the type of meeting and what the purpose is, you can even just start by appreciating them as a group. Be sure to recognize them for specific things.

A common thing for small business owners is to allow a lack of performance to cause resentment. Although you may want to let them know how you feel in a group setting, it never works. Praise in public, discipline in private. If you can't find *anything* to praise anyone for, you have a leadership problem.

There have been times when we had an entire meeting on appreciation. Each person appreciates another team member for something specific. We call it an "appreciation fest." Be sure that everyone is recognized. If anyone is left out, you'll have the opposite effect.

What Meetings Should You Have?

Daily Production Meeting

If you have production staff like technicians, or people who build or ship the product, you want to meet with them daily. Why? Because there is one thing that's on the mind of most typical production workers: *What's going on at home?* They're thinking about what they need to do (or want to do) when they get home. They're glued to their text messages or Facebook.

It's the job of the operations manager to hold this meeting every day to communicate how we are tracking on the vision, mission, and purpose. This meeting should take place every business day! This gets the production staff focused on the goal for the day. It doesn't have to be a long meeting. It can be 10 to 20 minutes. But the idea of production workers coming in and going straight to work with no leadership and no attitude adjustment is not leadership.

Here's a simple outline for your daily production meeting:

1. Recognition (see previous page).

2. Have a motivational quote or article that helps shape the values you want. For example, you can use Dale Carnegie's *Golden Booklet* (see www.DaleCarnegie.com) or John Maxwell's *365 Daily Reader,* or Zig Ziglar's *Little Book of BIG Quotes.* We have used all of these things and currently play five minutes of "A Conversation with Zig Ziglar." He shares a couple dozen values on video. Teaching your staff about values will help them be more productive and positive.

3. Have a technical tidbit of the day. Maybe something you learned at a seminar, or a best practice. Let your employees share also.

4. Go over any special instructions for the day or any company announcements. If you have service tickets or routes, pass those out.

Weekly Manager Meeting

If you're big enough to have managers, meet with them every week. For example, in my service company, I have a manager over each of the areas of business (Marketing, Sales, Operations, Administration). You may have one manager over some or all of that. Here's what's covered in that meeting:

1. Recognition.

2. Leadership training - Spend five minutes going over a section of this chapter.

3. Review reports - See Administration for the reports you need to be producing. These reports show how you are doing on your goals.

4. Go over any issues that need discussion or decisions.

Weekly Department Meetings

The manager of each department (Marketing, Sales, Operations and Administration) which may be you, should meet with those who are doing the work at least once a week.

1. Recognition.

2. Review reports. Example: If you are meeting with the Marketing Department, review the Sales by Source Report.

3. Training tidbit.

4. Discuss any issues surrounding performance or development of that area.

Weekly Staff Meeting

This is your big meeting where you have the entire staff together. It is important for your staff to see the team as one. Production staff tend to think that office people sit around with their feet on the desk eating chocolates all day, and the office staff may think the production staff isn't trying hard enough, or whatever. There are many assumptions that are made. Bringing the team together to show the importance of each team member's role is essential.

1. Start with positive client comments. Recognize those who met their goals. *Everyone* in the company has a goal. Deal with the negative client comments in private with those who are involved.

2. Recognize new employees. I am very cruel as I make the brand-new person recite the mission statement at the first staff meeting. After the new person recites it in the staff meeting, we discuss what it means. We have five pages on what our mission means. Those five pages are the first pages of our company manual.

3. Review sales report. You should have a monthly goal, and you should track it and post it every day.

4. Training session. This is training that benefits the entire group. It could be a DISC Assessment, a video on values from me, Zig Ziglar videos, technical training, or sales training.

As with any relationship, *regular communication* is the key to keeping everyone positive and productive.

Outside Educational Events

Educating your staff on technical as well as customer service, personal development, and leadership yields phenomenal returns, but most small business (and large companies) don't do this very well. I mentioned the little island on the Great Barrier Reef earlier. Just a little bit of training would have gone a long way to improve the service I received there.

At a recent hotel stay I talked to a new bellman who was handling my luggage and asked him what kind of training he had received. He said he was walked around the hotel and shown where things are located. That's it? The manager of that hotel is asleep at the wheel. This was a nice hotel connected to a beautiful convention center. It doesn't cost that much to have a few meetings like the ones mentioned here to transfer values. Obviously the values are missing at the top and therefore not shared because they don't exist!

I say take it beyond the meetings mentioned. Send your staff to outside educational events. It may feel like a challenge to spend the money to send an employee to a class or to a seminar. Not only does the seminar cost money, you lose production, and the amazing thing is your employees want to get paid while at the class! Then shortly after the seminar, they quit! At this point, you've got to ask yourself a Zig Ziglar question: "Is it better to train them and lose them, or *not* train them and keep them?"

My experience has been that having my staff attend educational events outside the office generates a huge return on investment. There may be things you can train them on in-house without investing a lot of money, but don't leave it at that.

Here are the benefits I've seen from sending employees to outside events:

Exposure to Experts

This is where you get leverage. Let an expert who has invested thousands of hours train my staff while I get other things done. Or better yet, we attend together so we can compare notes and share the experience.

Exposure to New Ideas

New ideas create vision, which creates desire. When our creativity is limited, our attitudes tend to be limited as well. Desire is the fuel of accomplishment. Desire is what increases action. Desire comes from vision—when you learn something new or an event takes place that changes your thinking. Some business owners who have limited thinking themselves don't want their employees getting new ideas because they may want to impose change which makes the owners uncomfortable.

Just because they get ideas doesn't mean you have to incorporate them, but on the other hand, it creates a situation where you don't have to do all the thinking. Are you finally getting the picture that the less you have to do the better? You don't have to use all the ideas. If you send your staff to an event that you don't attend, encourage them to take notes and bring back ideas to discuss. Take them to lunch or have a meeting at the office and go over the ideas. You can select the ones you want, they still feel valued and you get the benefit of using someone else's brain power!

A Feeling of Importance

Speaking of feeling valued, when you invest in educating your staff, it tells them they are important. They are valued. They are assets rather than expenses. Put education into your budget and use the phenomenal marketing systems to generate the income you need to fund it.

A Sense of Community

This is my favorite benefit. Phenomenal leadership is creating a community. A community of people with a shared vision, a shared mission, and a shared purpose. A community of people who support one another and operate by the same set of values. When you travel with your staff members or attend events together, you can bond with them and share the vision, mission, and purpose. This is your opportunity to make a difference in their lives and get to know them better.

You might think, *I'll go to the seminar myself and then transfer the knowledge I get to my staff when I return.* How is that working for you? It helps, but there's a big chasm between what you are able to transfer and what they *could* be getting. Between the time it takes for you to regurgitate it and re-teach it, not to mention the details you don't recall, it becomes so watered down that they are missing about 95 percent of it.

It has been said that the average attendee forgets 77 percent of what they learn at a seminar. This can be demonstrated by watching a movie you've seen a few times. Did you see a scene or a line that you thought you never saw previously? You bet! You might get the key point of the seminar, and that's great, but you leave a ton of good information on the table.

It can also be demonstrated with the game "telephone" in which one person whispers a message to another, which is passed through a line of people until the last player announces the message to the entire group. Errors typically accumulate in the retellings, so the statement announced by the last player differs significantly, and often amusingly, from the one uttered by the first.

Some players also deliberately alter what is being said in order to guarantee a changed message by the end of it (that would never happen in your business, right? Wrong!).

Keeping your team engaged in a learning environment keeps them focused on the right things. The old saying goes "An idle mind is the devil's workshop." When they are not engaged in learning, they begin to focus on the obstacles and problems. They will focus on the scuttlebutt, the water cooler conversation, or worse. When they are engaged in learning, you automatically begin to develop a better vision for the future. New ideas begin to emerge from the students. Your employees begin to give you constructive ideas rather than complaints.

Dale Carnegie said, "People support a world they help create."

I think one of my most important assets is the fact that I involve my people in developing the vision for the future. In fact, one of my employees was with me when the vision for Phenomenal Products was born. This doesn't mean that you will always agree or that things will always turn out exactly like you want them to, but getting your employees involved in the "vision casting" is huge.

Other benefits of taking employees to outside events:

1. A great time out of the office with the boss = stronger one-on-one relationships (if we treat them right on the trip and we remain a good example!).

2. An opportunity to see how they operate outside of work.

3. Exposure to the industry at large. I think we underestimate the power in this because we have been so overexposed.

4. Positions your company in your employees' minds as the expert company because you are not only investing in education, but investing in theirs as well.

5. Exposure to new ideas and techniques.

Remember that Experiential Marketing is important with your "internal clients" as well. Remember that you are leading a movement—a group of people who are on a mission together. Education is a humongous part of that.

You want your employees to do things the right way so long that they don't even *know* what the wrong way is anymore. That is not always possible, so when you see that they are getting off track begin to coach them and mentor them on a daily basis until they are back on track.

How to Find Phenomenal People

What kind of person are you looking for as an employee? In my seminars, I ask small business owners what they are looking for. Typically this is what the list looks like.

- Successful - someone who has done well in the past.

- Good work ethic - someone who isn't lazy.

- Positive attitude - someone with a pleasing personality and is enthusiastic.

- Great appearance - someone who dresses well and grooms themselves well.

- Intelligent - someone who is smart and can figure things out.

- Honest and trustworthy - one you can trust to do right by others.

- Loyal - one who is not there just for the money, but believes in your vision, mission, and purpose.

- Takes initiative - one who doesn't have to be told what to do every time.

- Organized - one who keeps track of their things and responsibilities, not absent-minded.

- A leader - one who will influence others positively.

Wow! We aren't asking for much are we? In today's "values challenged" world (I'm being nice), this is like finding a needle in a haystack!

What kind of person are they looking for as an employer?

- Successful - successful people want to associate with successful people.

- Good work ethic - they don't want to work for someone who is lazy.

- Positive attitude - who wants to work for someone with a negative attitude?

- Great appearance - well groomed people don't like to be associated with a sloppy leader.

- Intelligent - what smart person wants to work for a dumb person?

- Honest and trustworthy - who wants to work for someone they don't trust?

- Loyal - who wants to work for someone who might dump them at the drop of a hat?

- Takes initiative - who wants to work for someone who doesn't know how to lead?

- Organized - organized people like organized people.

- A leader - leaders don't want to work for someone who doesn't have leadership skills.

Have you noticed a pattern here? *You attract who you are.* This is why it is so important for you to become a different, better person. *If you are going to attract phenomenal people, you've got to be one!*

The phenomenally successful person builds the phenomenally successful business. Successful people don't want to work with someone who doesn't have a clear vision. They don't want to be on a mediocre mission, and they desperately want to have meaning in their lives. What is *your reputation* as a business owner? How do you rate in these areas?

Full Time, Part Time, Outsource?

Do you really need a full-time employee? I have found that a number of tasks on the implementation level of the organizational chart can be done by part timers. For example, I have part time people who make outgoing phone calls, who visit referral sources, and perform data entry. Depending on the type of business, you might even consider using a virtual assistant. You can outsource a number of things as well.

As mentioned previously, one of the most helpful things to understand as a leader is behavior and communication styles. There are a number of assessments available. As explained earlier, DISC is a very simple one, but has been very helpful to me and has been very helpful in getting my staff to communicate well with one another. Another one we use that is more comprehensive is the Birkman Method.

Finding Phenomenal Team Members

I often say that all of business and all of life is about relationships. Relying on ads to attract strangers is not the most phenomenal way to get new team members. As a small business owner, the most valuable skill you can develop is your ability to build a network of relationships. Not just with prospects, but with people in all areas of the community.

Recruiting Team Members is a Marketing Process!

When recruiting team members, you want to use the same processes you learned in Phenomenal Marketing Systems. You must *position* yourself in the community as the preferred employer by the way you interact in the community. The way you do that is by always looking professional, acting professional, and being positive and enthusiastic. When people ask you how you are doing, you say "PHENOMENAL!" They will wonder what you are smoking when you are always positive, but it has an effect.

It is strange to me that people notice what I consider to be small things. For example, on the voicemail recording for my cell phone, I close by saying, "Have a phenomenal and outstanding day" in a very enthusiastic voice. You won't believe how many comments I get from that small thing. When people ask me how I'm doing, I say, "Well, phenomenal of course!" Or I say, "I'm doing phenomenal, that's my job!" Like many things, I learned this from Zig. When you ask most people how they are doing (in Australia, it's, "How you going?"), the answer is usually "Good."

That wasn't good enough for Zig. He answered with "Better than good! But improving!" This is the kind of positive attitude you want to have to attract the right people. You want to attract positive people, not negative ones. Don't tell people in the community about your problems or complain about the economy. And above all, never complain about your work or your clients! When you do that, you're going to attract miserable people!

When you display a positive attitude, you attract people who want to be positive. Yesterday I came across a journal from many years ago. We were having problems with my son, I was in the midst of firing my bookkeeper, we had cash flow problems, I was tired and traveling too much, and my success was hit and miss on the road. I was frustrated. But I continued to trust in God, and I continued to display a positive attitude. Hope for the future will help you have the right attitude. You can have tremendous problems but still display a positive attitude. It helps you because it keeps you from going into despair, which will cause you to make irrational decisions. You've got to keep your head *and* your heart about you. Display a positive attitude even in the midst of tremendous problems.

When you see people you think might be good team members for you, talk to them about it even if you don't need anyone yet. You don't wait until you need a customer to start marketing, right? I hope not! Hopefully you are always marketing to keep your funnel full. The same is true in this case. Always be building relationships with people and attracting people so you will have a number of people to choose from when the time comes.

Kenny Pelletier is one of my inside sales reps and has been with us for over a decade. I knew Kenny from church, and every time there was a church function, I would talk to Kenny. He loved his job as a disc jockey at a Christian radio station, but they didn't pay him enough. "How are things going with you and your company?" he would ask. "Phenomenal, of course! You should join the team," I would reply. At that time, I didn't have an opening for Kenny. But I knew two things: One, it would take Kenny awhile to make a decision, and by that time something would probably open because were growing. And two, I knew anything could happen the next day.

You need to recruit before you need someone.

Kenny's daughter Elise began working with us when she was 18. She is a phenomenal team member who has filled many roles with excellence. She referred her then boyfriend (now husband), Santiago. How was I to know that this skinny, long-haired kid would become such a gift to me? How was I to know that this young man would be one of the most talented, positive, gifted, and loyal employees ever? How did I know he would become a "little Howard" as he teaches my programs at Phenomenal Products just as I would?

I didn't. But I did and do know that all of business is about relationships. This is one of the reasons I hire family members. Conventional wisdom says don't do it and that is because they don't understand how to be real and upfront about the business relationship—that it is separate from the personal relationship. They have to be okay with the decision if I have to let their family member go, even if they don't agree with it. Yes, there is a downside to hiring family. When they go on vacation, they generally go together! When there is a birth, sickness, or death, there goes the whole family. But, think about this. Because you are close to the family, these times can be the most meaningful to them when you are there to support them.

I have had situations where I had to fire two family members on the same day. It was hard but justified. I have also had a difficult situation where I had to severely discipline a family member and I couldn't discuss the situation with the other family members because they aren't in management. With all of that said, I still believe the positives far outweigh the negative.

After Mary Ann came onboard with us, her husband and son ended up working with us. Their family is like our family. Daniel is like a son to me. Mary Ann has helped us in a variety of roles, her husband Mark was our top sales rep before starting his own business. Daniel started with us when he was only 18 and served as my operations manager for three years.

Jim Bardwell was my special referral marketing agent who helped me implement my referral marketing systems. He was with me for eight years and did practically everything in my company before taking up that role. I met Jim at an industry networking group and my positive attitude is what attracted him to me. His words were, "Whatever that man has, I want!" (by the way, this was the same group of negative guys who laughed at me and asked me, "Who do you think you are, Zig Ziglar or somebody?"). Of course Jim was one of the few positive people in the group, and we really hit it off.

He and his wife invited me out for dinner and asked me for a job. He was working for a competitor, and I told him that I would have to call the owner and ask permission; and second, I didn't have a position. He told me he was leaving the other company regardless, and as fate would have it, I had to fire a guy the next morning. Jim came onboard and not only helped me take my company to the next level, he also became one of my best friends in the entire world. He has been one of my biggest cheerleaders. At lunch one day after being laughed at by the other guys, he looked across the table and told me, "I *do* see you as the Zig Ziglar of our industry." A tear rolled down my cheek because little did Jim know that what I am doing now was a hidden dream of mine.

Jim now works with one of my first Phenomenal Products clients, John Browning, who is also one of my coaches and also one of my best friends and biggest supporters. This is what is possible! This is why it is worth building a phenomenal team!

I briefly mentioned Scott and Dennis previously. Scott came aboard as a partner way back in 1997. I had met him at an industry function, too, and we played golf together once and awhile. Well, I should say that Scott played golf. I finally realized that whatever I was doing out there on the golf course wasn't actually "playing golf," it was more like the ball was playing "hide and seek." As we tooled around the course, we talked about the ultimate service company and what it would look like.

We took on another partner as well. Dennis was also a colleague who was in some groups where I networked. The three of us had a great eight-year run in many ways, although we made tons of mistakes and built up a lot of debt. Finally Scott bailed, and soon after Dennis and I collided. Dennis went on to do training, which is what he loved. After a stint working with one of our vendors, Scott came back to work with me and now manages the Administration Department for all of my companies.

What you need to notice is that all of these people came from *networking*. I'll say it again, your most valuable skill as a business owner is the ability to build a large network of phenomenal relationships. All of business is about relationships.

My first and second employee were both with me about 20 years. The only reason they didn't stay with me was due to a lack of phenomenal leadership systems. We went through some periods when I was absent and the management team I had in place wasn't getting the job done.

When you think about the Phenomenal Marketing Systems for clients, think about it also in terms of attracting and acquiring the best employees. Earlier you learned about positioning yourself as the only obvious choice for your niche market. You must position yourself as the obvious choice as an employer. You learned about referral marketing. Building your network and offering a reward for a new employee works well.

Client-based marketing—start with your existing team members. We offer a $300 reward for a new hire. $100 when they are successfully hired, $100 when they have been with us 90 days, and $100 when they've been employed for six months.

Direct Advertising and Internet Advertising would personally be my last choices for finding potential employees because I want to know someone who actually *knows* this person. Michelle worked at a retail store that was closing, and my wife happened to frequent the store. My wife referred the manager of the store to me, who was not the right fit; but he referred Michelle who was a manager under him. When someone refers someone who works under them that highly, pay attention!

Phenomenal Compensation

One of the frequently asked questions I get as a business coach is, "How do I pay my people so they will perform?" The answer, "You don't." Studies have revealed that employees rate their pay behind four other more important factors, such as 1) how they are treated, 2) whether they feel "in" on things, 3) their benefits, and 4) work environment.

They may not verbalize this and may not even be aware of it, but the fact remains that people stay because they feel they belong and you are adding value to them. Of course you do have to pay them well; and if you don't handle this part right, you can have serious problems.

Many conflicts seem to arise over money-related issues, but my contention is that the conflict is actually due to a lack of communication. Be very clear and upfront with your employees about pay issues.

How you pay is just as important as how much you pay. If you have the right person in place who is onboard with the vision, mission, and purpose, you can pay many ways and still get results. Some positions require more incentive or performance-based pay to increase production.

Here are some pointers:

1. Determine how much the position is worth. You do this by referring to your 12-month budget to determine how much you will invest in the position.

2. Determine what impact the position can have on profits. Can this position up-sell? Can it affect gross profits? Can it make or cost a sale? Does this position generate prospects?

3. Break it down. I prefer to pay an hourly base and give bonuses on extraordinary performance.

My good friend Ellen Rohr says, "If they bring it in on time and on budget, they get to stay. If they bring it in early and under budget, share the gain with them." This creates a game that's fun to play.

Keep the team informed of the score, and work together to create strategies. In my service company, we post the sales numbers daily. They celebrate successes and rally at the last minute if we're behind to pull it out. We offer a number of bonuses to foster that, but it's all in the budget.

When we do events at Phenomenal Products, the staff works really hard and really long. I always share some extra dough with them for that. They would work hard every event, but this ensures that they're watching the numbers as closely as I am.

So the bottom line of pay systems is to treat them right, recognize them, give them benefits, create a positive working environment. Pay them well on top of that and you will be on your way to phenomenal leadership!

The Application Process

Before interviewing someone, have the person fill out an application. You can get employment applications from a variety of sources for your state. You want to have a system for this that doesn't require you to be involved.

Since it's a sales process, I don't like to break the connection. If this person is desirable, other people are going to be after him or her too, so you need to act quickly on the application and interview process. Go slowly from there; this is "setting the hook," so to speak. Once you bait the hook, you don't jerk too quickly, or you'll yank the bait out of the mouth of the fish, you'll bring in the wrong fish, or you'll damage the good fish.

Have a simple application procedure where any employee can give the applicant the required paperwork for your state, a copy of the person's driver's license, and so on. If you don't have employees or an office, consider a verbal application or online submission form and check it often so you can set the hook. Once the application is completed, and you have the drug screening authorization, etc., you can review the application to see if he or she qualifies for the position.

If you are at the office when the candidate comes in, observing the behavior may give you an idea if this person is a good candidate or not (remember the pot-smoking guy I spoke about earlier). If you want to interview the person at that time, you can set the hook.

Phenomenal Interviewing

Remember that acquiring "internal clients" is a marketing process. You have recruited them, now this is the first "sales call." You are going to qualify them and they are going to qualify you, just like in a sales process.

You may or may not have met them before. What is their first impression of you? As I shared in Phenomenal Operations Systems, people make eleven assumptions about you in the first 30 seconds of meeting you—before you even open your mouth!

You want them to see you as the one and only person they would work with, just like you want your prospects to feel that same way. So be sure to follow these steps:

Be prepared.

Review the application. Have your questions ready. Don't multitask. Don't be in a hurry. This is a very important event as it will set the tone for the entire employment experience. Make sure your office is neat and organized. No one you want working for you wants to work for a slob. If you don't have an office, meet at Starbucks or someplace like that.

Observe.

Was the candidate on time? Remember, this is probably the best you will see. How are they dressed? How are they groomed? Any quirks that would cost you sales? Is the person's handshake weak? Too strong?

Ask open-ended questions.

Avoid "yes" and "no" questions unless you are just confirming information. Let them talk! One of the biggest mistakes in interviewing and sales is talking too much. Listen, listen, listen! Listen to the person's responses and pay attention to whether he or she is making eye contact or not. Is the person confident? Too confident? Cocky?

There are many questions and many programs you can attend to learn more about this interviewing process, but I have been successful with a few basic questions:

- How are you today?

- Tell me about yourself…

- I see that you are applying for <position>?

- I see you are/were working at…

- What did you like?

- What didn't you like?

- Why do you want to work here?

- Why should I hire you over someone else?

- Do you have reliable transportation? (It's illegal to ask if they own a car.)

- Do you have a valid driver's license?

- Do you have a clean driving record?

If you feel you want to hire this person, share the opportunity with him or her. Begin by effectively communicating your vision, mission, and purpose. One of the things I do is let the person know that there is a simple two-part agreement that is important for us to work together:

Part one is that we care about their dreams and goals. Here's what I say: Other companies may treat you like a number and devalue you as a "human resource," but we care about you as a person. We want to put you on a track to reach your goals and dreams. We've created a system where you can grow and you can write your own check.

Part two is that we can't provide that without reaching the company goals: The company has goals, a mission, and a purpose. We have systems that we operate by. When you help us implement those systems and fulfill the mission, we can help you reach your goals and dreams. Otherwise we can't.

At this point, you will then go over:

- Job description

- Pay plan

- Benefits

- Work hours

- And anything else the person would need to know to make the decision. You may want to conduct additional interviews or get your team involved in the interview process before you make the hire.

Phenomenal Orientation

Orientation is a very important process for a successful employment experience. Think about how a brand-new employee feels when they join a brand-new team. Your job as a leader is to make sure the new hire comes aboard successfully. All of your staff should be trained on how to treat one another, and someone should have the responsibility of sharing the company culture with the new person.

Since leadership is effectively communicating your vision (and values), mission, and purpose, and the most powerful factor in an organization is its *culture,* this needs to start on day one of employment. If this is not specifically and strategically managed, you will end up with a different culture from the one you want. A specific orientation process designed to introduce a new hire into the culture and to share the vision, mission, and values of the organization is key.

The time frame will vary depending on what kind of business you have, but a full day would be ideal. And if you are the positive, enthusiastic, leader you should be, it would be phenomenal for you to do it. At least until you get your entire team so steeped in your culture that they don't know any other way.

I know this can sound like a huge burden, but other than getting money in the front door, there is nothing more important. In fact, if you don't get your team right, they can ultimately determine how much money comes in and how much goes out the back door!

Schedule it.

If you absolutely cannot do it, at least take the time to train a model employee to be a trainer and have them do it. *Do not* let just any employee do this important task. Even a good employee can say something wrong. It may be an innocent gesture said out of nervousness. This is the first impression of working at your company. It should be outstanding. The idea is that the person is officially welcomed to the team and he or she feels the love of the community.

The following is a sample of what could be included in Orientation Day:

Welcome to the team.

If you have daily production meetings or the person starts on your weekly staff meeting day, introduce the person in front of the group. Otherwise, walk him or her around and introduce to each person individually. Say something nice about each team member you introduce them to. This causes your new employee to look up to that person and value them at a high level. If your team member doesn't deserve that, they shouldn't be there! This also gives your new hire a great feeling as he or she observes the positive enthusiasm.

Go over Vision, Mission, and Purpose.

This includes everything we talked about in the previous section. One of the things I did when I became turnkey was to record a DVD that outlined the vision and values, mission, and purpose as well as an orientation on our basic processes. This was helpful for them to see the equipment and processes before actually handling them.

Share the Organizational Chart.

This shows the new hire how the team fits together and shows the importance of every role.

The following items may have been covered in the interview process, but they need to be reviewed again on orientation day. You want to make sure there are no miscommunications early on.

- Go over position description. Make sure the person understands *what* they will be responsible for, even though they may not know *how* yet.

- Review pay plan.

- Review benefits.

- Review work hours.

- Issue uniforms and tools.

- Review dress code policy.

- Issue and go over Employee Handbook. You want to be very clear about the basic on-time policies, compensation policies, social media policies, etc.

- Go over safety guidelines.

Ninety-Day Probationary Period.

Check with your labor attorney about establishing a 90-day probationary period for new hires. This will be the best performance you will see. Are they on time? Good attitude? Are they catching on? Are they learning?

Phenomenal Training Systems

Training is the key to developing good habits, instilling confidence, and preparing people to grow to the next level. Most small business owners don't train their staff properly. There are many reasons—yours may include the following. Perhaps you're too busy working "in" the business to do it yourself. You don't have someone qualified to train someone else. It's expensive. And worse, if you've invested a lot of money and time into someone and then they marched straight to the competition for better pay, you probably have a bad taste in your mouth.

If you think it's expensive and painful to train people only to have them leave you, consider again this question by Zig Ziglar: "Is it better to *train* them and lose them, or *not* train them and *keep* them?"

I think we know the answer to that one. Get the negative emotion off the playing field on this one. Understand that training is the key. Not only the technical training they need to do their job, but training on customer service and personal development is key. In fact, character training is the most important training of all. If we have character, everything else will follow. We will do right by others, and we will want to better ourselves.

We use a variety of materials from Ziglar to train our staff on personal development and sales. We use my materials to train them on customer service, and of course you want to develop in-house training programs for your technical work.

You can bring in outside trainers in your industry and take your staff to training events. If there is a program complete enough in your industry with step-by-step manuals, you may be able to bypass the entire process of writing procedures in certain areas of your business. For example, in my service company, we have an outside group that developed training curriculum in a specific area with a manual that goes with it. That department goes to Dallas twice a year and we use their manual as our procedures.

Many times an outside training program will have procedures that you don't need or won't be robust enough, but you can use them as your templates and build on them. When you can utilize programs that are already done, you can save yourself a lot of time.

Training Principles

There's an old saying for presentations that goes like this:

- Tell them what you are going to teach them.

- Teach them.

- Tell them what you taught them.

Training is about repetition and creating habits out of learning.

Another saying is:

- Tell

- Show

- Watch

In other words: *Tell* them what to do. *Show* them how to do it. *Watch* them do it until they are doing it consistently. This is where most trainers fail. They don't invest enough time actually letting the trainee do the process.

Tell

This is what is called the "cognitive" learning domain. For this you need a *teacher*. This is about *information*. If you are learning to fly an airplane, there will be some classroom (or video) time or time reading a manual, which is important because you need to know the *information*.

Show

This is what is called the "psychomotor" learning domain. For this you need an *instructor*. This is about building *skill*. You aren't going to really learn to fly just with information. You need to develop your *skill*.

Watch

This is called the "affective" learning domain. For this you need to create experiences. This is about the trainee getting *experience*. You aren't going to be a phenomenal pilot without experience. Once your trainee has the skill, you need to allow him or her to get *experience* (in a controlled environment). This is where the right habits and the character will truly be built.

The KISS Principle

No, I'm not talking about the rock band (but wearing make-up and getting into character *is* a phenomenal way to teach!). KISS stands for: Keep It Simple Sam.

You thought I was going to offend you, didn't you? Avoid giving too much information at one time. The human mind can only absorb a certain amount of information in one period. The more important thing is to practice the new information. Remember that training is about building habits.

When we train someone on a new process, we break it down into bite-size chunks. For example, in my service company when we hire a new service person, he or she starts with Orientation, which gives them the vision, mission, and purpose, and the basic policies. To help the person learn the procedures, we break it down to one procedure per day. Then each day we refer to the previous procedures and add a new one to it.

Think of baking a cake. We start by understanding what kind of cake we are baking. We have a picture of what it should look like and taste like. We know what flavor it is (this is your vision, mission, and purpose). Now we get out all the ingredients for making a successful cake (these are our values and our basic policies that ensure we live out our values and develop the culture we want). In fact, a great pastry begins with the right culture.

Then we have the steps of actually creating the cake. These are our procedures. Here's how long you bake the cake, how long it has to cool (and why), how to mix the frosting. The procedures are the how. Remember to connect the procedures to the why (vision, mission, and purpose).

Once I have baked a few cakes in the presence of my trainer, I can now bake a cake successfully on my own. The more experience I get at baking cakes, and baking different cakes, the more it will help me to become a phenomenal cake maker.

Give constant feedback. Don't let the cake burn in the oven because you don't want to micromanage or you want to "teach them a lesson." Don't let too much time lapse between practice. Repetition is the "mother" of learning. "Within 30 days, people forget 90 percent of what they have learned unless it is repeatedly reinforced," says Professor Albert Mehrabian, UCLA.

If you have a trainee who isn't catching on, you must determine whether it is an *attitude* or an *aptitude* issue. Is the person the right fit for the position? Is your company suited for them? Did you make a bad hire? Or do you just need to do more training?

Phenomenal Delegating

When you are delegating something outside of your team member's job description, there are some principles and steps I think will help you. When delegating a task that you haven't specifically trained someone on, follow these steps.

First, be clear about the outcome. Keep the different communication styles in mind. Be sure to over-communicate when delegating. And remember the reason you are delegating. The reason you are delegating a task is so you can multiply your output. This frees you up to do other important things to reach the vision, mission, and purpose.

You want the person to take full ownership of the task. You are there to guide and coach, but if you have to micromanage it, there isn't a reason to delegate it. An unpopular but very effective technique is called "benign neglect." In other words, you intentionally become unavailable at times. This trains your staff not to rely on you for every single thing they need. Now you certainly would not do this if they did not have what they needed in the way of procedures, tools, and support. And someone needs to be in charge in case of an emergency or a breakdown in systems. That does not always have to be you. You can also set it up so only a certain person or persons knows how to contact you and where you are.

Another mistake made in delegating is "buying it back." In other words you give your employee a task that he or she finds difficult. The mistake many managers make is that they take it back and say, "I'll handle it myself." Even though there may be times that is appropriate, don't make that a habit because it teaches your employees that if it is hard, they can just give it back to you.

Rather, it is very healthy to help them work through a difficult task, and they will eventually adopt that value system in the future. When they have difficulty, ask, "What are *you* going to do about it?" At first they may say, "Me?" You then explain why you want them to work on it instead of you, and that you know they can do it.

There are also cases in which your delegates don't really understand what it is that you want. In this case, rephrase, and refocus your instructions in different ways for different communication styles so they understand. This is a natural process due to different communication styles, behavior styles, and personalities. Don't feel that something is wrong if you have to do this sometimes.

Daily or weekly reporting and checklists are great ways to keep everyone on track. I meet with my team once a week to make sure our projects are moving forward. You may want to keep a running list on a simple Word document, you may want to use email, or a handwritten to-do list that is checked off and returned to you. Make sure you have a follow-up system such as this to make sure your delegations don't get lost in a black hole. Having a follow-up system to recap progress also helps you to keep from overloading your employees. Between their job description, which may have a checklist of daily duties and their to-do list, you can get a clear picture of their load.

Phenomenal Coaching Systems

The goal of Phenomenal Leadership Systems is to develop a community that has completely bought into your vision, mission, and purpose. They know their position and exactly what to do every day. But the reality is that human beings will miss the mark for one reason or another, and most leaders, managers, and supervisors don't know how to handle it in a responsible, positive manner.

All team members (including you) have developed their own ways of solving conflicts over a lifetime. We must teach them our protocol for communicating, and it is especially important when dealing with them about performance or attitude issues.

Disciplinary Principles

Always discipline in private. I have made the mistake of bringing something negative up publicly many times and it *never* works out right. Even if I don't mention a name, there is a negative reaction that decreases performance instead of increasing it.

It's *always* about the vision, mission, and purpose. Always. Keep your focus on the performance as it relates to those three things. In the event of theft, lying, sexual harassment, drug or alcohol abuse at work, and things of that nature, they are immediately released. The following doesn't apply in that case.

Determine the difference between *desired* performance and *actual* performance by *asking questions!* Just like sales, asking questions is the very best way to get people to "own" something. In this situation, you are selling ideas and concepts and you want them to "own" their behavior. So the selling process is the same. Ask good questions.

Ask questions like these:

- "Can you tell me about (whatever the situation is)?" This question brings attention to the issue without judgment. There may be things you are unaware of. I've made assumptions in the past that were incorrect and judged people before they even had an opportunity to explain. Once I knew the actual circumstances, it turned out they didn't do anything wrong.

- "Do you understand that this is your responsibility?"

- "Do you know how to do it?"

- "Do you have the resources you need to accomplish it?"

- "Do you have the time to do it?" Many times they will use this as the excuse, so you can go back to the training and go over how they are using their time to determine if this is a legitimate issue or not.

Sometimes it's a systems issue. If the system has been changed or the work flow has changed since the system was developed, a systems change may be needed. There may be issues with the system or things that others are doing that are affecting the outcome. I need to know that.

Determine whether it is an *attitude* issue or an *aptitude* issue.

Once I have covered the questions about knowing their job and having the time and resources to do it, and I have considered whether I have the wrong behavior style in that position, I need to explore whether or not the person is having an attitude challenge. I might ask, "Is everything okay?" Sometimes, there are personal issues at home or with relationships that get in the way of work. Sometimes people develop addictions or have financial problems. Hopefully these will surface before you have to get into a disciplinary situation because you are really always coaching and leading, but sometimes they don't surface until later. Usually because the supervisor isn't paying enough attention to pick up on the situation. Since I am a turnkey business owner, I rely on my managers and supervisors to warn me that something is amiss or someone is veering in the wrong direction.

Get their *agreement* to change.

Once I have covered these things, I will ask a final question: "Are you willing to get this done in the way it is supposed to be done?" If the response is in the positive, I shake the person's hand, look him or her in the eye and say, "Great! I'm counting on you." By the way, the eye contact and handshake is very important because the person is giving you his or her word to change. And your words of expectation should be positive. Avoid the feeling to say something degrading. That tendency shows you don't value them at the level that you should.

If we have to visit the issue again or other issues come up, we go into a formal disciplinary process that ends up with the person being restored, quitting, or being released.

Once you enter into a formal disciplinary process, you want to have a witness, and you should record everything in writing. Please note that none of what is written in this book is legal advice and shouldn't be construed as such. Please consult a labor attorney before using any of the disciplinary principles in this book.

At this point, we either have a serious aptitude issue and they need training or to be moved to another area, or we have an attitude issue. If you have exhausted all of the issues and you feel that they just don't want to do it for some reason, or their personal distractions have come to an unmanageable place, you will need to address it.

Ask this question, "Are we the right fit for you?" In other words, don't tell the person you don't think *he or she* is the right fit. If you are requiring a high level of commitment in work and attitude, they may not be up to it. It may not be the right fit. And that is okay, because you have developed a phenomenal leadership system that consistently attracts and keeps the very best staff members. There is no room for those who aren't ready to play at that level.

The Value of Daily Coaching and Mentoring

People are creatures of habit. We love routine. We hate change. Your employees develop work habits, and they develop them quickly. Before long, they are in a routine. Sometimes the *wrong* routine! When we hire people, we prefer them with no experience. The reason is that they have built habits that they won't change.

The key is to get your employees started off the right way, and to coach and mentor them daily. If there is a change of procedure, then you must not only tell them and show them, but you must also *inspect* them on a daily basis. *Expect* only what you *inspect!* It is very true. If you are not watching what is going on, people seem to drift. If you drift just a little over a long period of time, it won't even look like the original procedure! It's like a copy of a copy of a copy of a copy. The most recent copy doesn't look like the master because it was not a copy of the master. It was a copy of a copy that had developed some imperfections.

If you draw a straight line all the way across a chalk board and then draw another one above it and point the line only a couple of degrees north, the end of the line will be a long way from the end of the straight line. It starts out only a couple of degrees off, but the farther you take the line, the farther off it is. It's the same with your employees. If they get off track a bit, over time the effect can be huge.

A bad habit is like a bad golf swing or an improper swing of a baseball bat. If you continue to use that swing, you will form a habit that is hard to break. Here's the scary part. If you are having fair success with that swing, you will be hesitant to change. Why? One reason is that it is uncomfortable. But another reason is the fear of loss. What if I do worse? The fear of loss is one of the most powerful motivator known to humankind. It's working, why change it?

In the case of an employee doing something the wrong way, even when we point out that we are losing money or emotional equity with our clients (your brand) or whatever, unless it is hurting their pocketbook, they may not have the motivation to change. They will be uncomfortable doing it a different way.

The way to change that mindset is with daily coaching and mentoring. Go over the procedure again and again. Drill your employees. And of course you must have written procedures and you must have already shown them how to do it and watched them do it. After that, you must reinforce the habit daily.

As mentioned previously: "Within 30 days, people forget 90 percent of what they have learned unless it is repeatedly reinforced." Ninety percent? Wow! It has to be repeatedly reinforced.

I want to remind you of something I have taught in my book *7 Secrets of a Phenomenal LIFE*. Every person has a "filtering process" when they are presented with a new idea that requests change on their part. These are "stages" that people go through. They filter the idea through their bank of experiences and values.

This is not something that is intentionally done. It is a subconscious process that manifests in action or inaction. In other words we do what we value deep down, regardless of what we say. We might say that we want to lose weight, but we take contrary action such as eating a bowl of ice cream right before we go to bed! Why? If we really wanted to lose weight, we wouldn't eat the ice cream right? The truth is that our subconscious value system wants something that takes precedent for the moment. It is a more urgent need. It is desperate to be filled. The problem is that we don't know what the real emotional need is, because it is buried, and we may never dig it up! So we eat the ice cream.

Now imagine if your personal trainer was sitting in your den with you. When you were tempted to eat the ice cream, the trainer reminded you of the real truth. The truth is that you don't really *need* the ice cream. It's an emotional need that cannot be fulfilled with ice cream. In fact, you are going to feel *worse* after eating the ice cream. Tomorrow morning you will feel badly, and it will affect your performance in other areas. So your coach, your mentor, your personal trainer helped you stay on track. You drink a large glass of water instead.

Obviously we cannot be with every employee every moment of the day, but we (or someone) can be in constant touch so there is enough interaction to keep people on track. A special note: This *will not* happen only by "telling" people what to do in meetings. To help them change habits, you have to be sitting in the den once and a while when the temptation to get the ice cream occurs.

The six steps in the "filtering" process are:

1. *Unawareness.* You just aren't aware that the concept is important.

2. *Awareness.* You become aware that it is important, but you haven't come to a place where you are willing to change.

3. *Willing to change.* Now you are willing, but you don't have the support or the "will power" to make it happen.

4. *Controlled attention.* Now you begin to get somewhere. Most of the time you do it right. Most nights you don't eat ice cream, but if you have a bad day, you might break down.

5. *Commitment.* This is the minimum level where you want all of your employees. At this level, you get consistency. It has to be an unusual situation where they would deviate. You would have had a monster of a day to give in to the ice cream.

6. *Characterization.* This is the ultimate level. At this level, you wouldn't eat the ice cream if someone had a gun to your head! You have come to a place where the value of health dramatically overrides your physical and emotional cravings. In fact, because you have thoroughly trained yourself, the old habit has been replaced with a new habit.

Understanding that everyone goes through this filtering process to build habits is important, and daily coaching and mentoring helps your team build the right habits.

The Write-Up

If you haven't been able to turn things around with coaching, it's time to begin the disciplinary process. Please understand that the goal of this process is to restore the person to performance. It is also important to have a paper trail in the file at this point. Refer to a labor attorney as it relates to all of these things. This is not legal advice.

Sit down with the employee with a witness. You need to have a formal document that describes the desired performance as it is outlined in the job description and the policies and procedures. Make notes of what you talked about and what the employee has agreed to. The document states that if you have to revisit a lack of performance within a specified period of time, the person will be given "Decision Making Leave."

Decision Making Leave is the opportunity for the person to take leave for one day (with pay) to decide whether to comply with the policies and procedures or to quit. My goal is to help the person quit so I don't have to release him or her.

If you maintain your Phenomenal Leadership Systems properly, you won't have to even get into this process. It will be a mutual agreement for the person to move on. But there are occasions when you have allowed people to stray or they refuse to grow or they make poor judgment calls, and you have to release them.

If he or she doesn't return to acceptable performance, you give the person leave (with pay) to make a decision whether your company is a good fit or not. It's okay if you aren't a good fit for the person. A phenomenally successful company is not for everyone. It takes a phenomenal attitude, hard work, and constant learning and stretching. Everyone doesn't want that.

Have the person take the day off and come back the next day with a decision to either comply or quit. If the person chooses to stay, he or she has only one more chance to get it right.

How to Release Someone and Remain Best Friends

This issue is probably the biggest reason small business owners don't build a team. The pain, agony, and potential outfall of firing someone is too much for them to imagine. It isn't easy. I've had to release people I loved.

One of my best friends in the world is Jim Bardwell. He was my special agent for eight years. He did practically everything in the company and eventually became my top referral marketing agent. He took that position to an entirely new level. He had the vision, mission, and purpose down to a science.

But after eight years together we both knew it was time for him to move on. In that case, it was a mutual, positive event. He is now living his dream in Nashville. He has found his groove and we have been blessed. This is the kind of outcome you want. The goal is for both of you to understand that the personal relationship is separate from the business relationship. It doesn't mean you don't have a personal relationship, it just means we understand that we might be best friends but can't work together. There are lots of people who work for my company with whom I don't have a personal relationship. And that's okay. It's not required. They fulfill the vision, mission, and purpose. And that is what is required.

I've had to release people for not performing, and I've had to release people who simply did things that were wrong and they deserved to be fired. No matter what the situation, it's never fun.

This is just another reason your dream has to be compelling. Sooner or later you'll have to endure ugly things for your business to grow. Having systems in your business—especially good leadership systems, will help you avoid much of the heartache; and when you do have to let someone go (or help them quit), it will be obvious to everyone that you did what's right. As the old saying goes, "A smooth sea doesn't make a great sailor."

So when it comes down to it, if you have done your coaching properly, it shouldn't be a surprise to the person, unless you find out about something that warrants termination. If that is the case, bring the person into your office with a witness and simply say, "Effectively immediately you are terminated from employment." Simple as that. Nothing more, nothing less. Accompany the person as he or she gathers personal belongings, or let the person know when he or she can come back with an appointment to get his or her personal belongings.

If you say anything more, you open yourself to an array of potential issues. It's best to cut it off just like that. If you have a personal relationship outside of work, you can preface it with "My goal is that our relationship outside of <Your Company Name> will continue to prosper, but effectively immediately you are terminated from employment." I have done this both ways and can tell you from experience that doing it any other way just hasn't worked in my experience.

The Greatest Leadership Message Ever

Across the United States small businesses and large corporations alike struggle with the same issues. Cut-throat competition that is selling "below invoice," customers who don't want to pay the advertised price, employees who don't want to do what management wants them to do, customer service is non-existent and management is frustrated because it doesn't have the resources needed due to a tight budget.

Employees don't care about the company and they don't care about the customer because they don't feel anyone cares about them. Companies think they can't afford the "luxury" of recruiting and training the right people, so mediocrity reigns. Many companies that fit this profile struggle to make a profit. The result is a frustrated management team, resentful workers, and disappointed customers.

While the typical business is warring over price, cutting budgets, and desperately trying to find "good" people, Starbucks has loyal customers standing in line happily paying $4 for a cup of coffee—a commodity that has been around since AD 1100 when Li Kau Fi brewed the first in China. (Or when John Coffee served up the first cup in England, whichever story you want to believe.)

Employees over at Southwest Airlines are on a fervent mission to make sure the company achieves its vision. They love the company so much they seem like multilevel evangelists. And Nordstrom continues to build upon their legendary customer service.

How have companies like this managed to rise above the mediocrity that rules in the typical company? Why is it that their employees *and* their customers love the company? What do these companies have in common (other than being extremely profitable)? Do they have something unique? Is it just great marketing? Is it just great management? Is there one simple concept that can bring all of the proven strategies of building a phenomenally successful business together?

The answer is found in the word *"community."*

A Longing for Belonging

What truly sets these companies apart is they have created "community" in their businesses. Community is a word that has many meanings for many people. We often refer to community in the context of our neighborhoods or our local area. We sometimes refer to groups of people as community—the Hispanic community, for example. We talk about the global community and even a virtual community as it relates to the Internet.

My definition of community goes much deeper than just a group of people or a neighborhood: community is the sense of belonging for which all humans hunger.

Every human being has a "longing for belonging." We are created that way. We have a need to be connected to other people. We have a deep desire to be part of something meaningful—something that makes a difference. The longing for community is the reason people join clubs. It also happens to be the reason people join gangs. Humans have the need to identify with a group of people who accept and love them. A group of people who belong to each other and walk through life with one another through victory and defeat.

The family is the first community that a person belongs to, but community as it once existed in the United States has all but vanished—the idea of having dinner as a family and being deeply involved in one another's lives, truly enjoying one another's successes and enduring one another's failures is a challenge. The idea of giving up our own rights to serve others—we have lost this essence of community in family; and therefore it does not exist in our businesses, churches, and institutions for the most part. Our organizations today mirror the way we live our independent lives.

Yet as we pursue our rugged independence and our individual rights, deep down we all long to experience community as we once did. The scarier part is that many of the younger people today (your new workforce), doesn't even know what community feels like!

Single parents, latch key kids who are now adults—they have not felt true community. They have not felt the love and encouragement that true community can bring. But they long for it. They may not even know what to call it or even how to explain it, but the feeling is definitely there. They need to be loved. They need to be accepted. They need to be recognized. They need to be part of something that means something. They have a longing for belonging.

Building Community in Your Business

If you understand and implement the principles of building community in your business, you will be able to do something for others that you may have never done before—help them experience the very thing they long for. The very thing every one of your employees desperately wants and needs—and will do almost anything to get. Your business can be the first place they ever truly feel connected and needed. You have the unique opportunity to give them the feeling of being part of something bigger than themselves. Your reward for that is your employees will begin to love your company for it. They will become your biggest evangelists, which in turn creates loyal, high-paying clients who increase your profits.

Keep in mind that your employees may not even know what they are looking for, but be assured they will know it when they feel it. When they experience community that you foster in your company, they will respond. There will be a few who won't, but if you do it right, it will be only a few, and that handful will quickly move on.

Finally, chances are you may not have experienced true community yourself. Chances are you are longing for true community and trying to fill that void with hobbies and business deals. If you do not understand and operate in community yourself, I can promise you that your people won't either. If you are not open and honest, they won't be either. If you are not committed to the vision and mission, they won't be either. If you talk badly about customers, they will too. As the owner or manager, you will have to partici-pate in community just as you expect your employees to participate.

Living in community and doing what is required won't be easy. If it was easy everyone would do it. The very reason that most companies are ordi-nary—mediocre, just getting by and complaining the whole way—is because they don't understand what community is and they won't commit to com-munity values even when they think they understand them. Too hard. Too difficult. Too much work for an intangible result.

But you, on the other hand, can rise above the mediocrity. You can expe-rience the exhilarating feeling of not only belonging to an extraordinary movement, but you will be at the helm. You will be recognized as the one who led the charge. The one who changes your business and changes your industry and has a profound and positive impact on many, many lives.

The only way you can begin to create a positive community—one that will give you what your clients and employees want—is to be transparent with one another and begin to develop "the way we do things here." Your community *system* includes your mission, your values, your goals, your pur-pose, and the policies and procedures of your culture.

If you think about the Amish community as an example, there is a cer-tain way they do things. Certain values they have. You may or may not agree with it, but that doesn't matter. What matters is that you create a compelling mission, vision, and purpose for your company and begin to craft the values you want to live out. Each step that is created in marketing, sales, and opera-tions of your business must be carefully crafted from the mission, vision, and values of your company.

Is it easy? No. But if you don't do it, someone else will define your com-munity experience for you, and that usually doesn't work out so well.

Chapter 10

The Number One Reason Most Small Businesses Don't Grow

(or do as well as they could)

I shared a Japanese proverb earlier that says, "Vision without action is just a daydream…." I was speaking to a group one time and my friend, Kirby Lammers who was in the audience, chuckled and muttered "FTI."

I asked him what it meant. He said a speaker he heard once called it "**F**ailure **T**o **I**mplement." Many times you know *what* to do and *how* to do it, you just *don't* do it. After coaching hundreds of business owners and addressing thousands, I have found that FTI is the number one reason that small businesses don't grow or do as well as they could.

Small business owners are so overwhelmed, distracted, and just trying to pay the bills that actually implementing anything additional can be daunting. This book is chock-full of phenomenal systems and strategies that can help your business; but if you don't use them, they obviously won't do you any good. These systems and strategies have literally revolutionized small businesses around the world, but it only happened because they overcame FTI.

So, what causes FTI, and how can you overcome it?

The Four Golden Keys to Implementation

Key #1: Inspiration

Have you noticed that the most successful small business owners are excited about the future? Have you noticed they are focused on the possibilities rather than just the problems? They see something others don't see. They have hope for the future because they *know* they can grow the business. They *know* they can improve their lives.

I call that *inspiration*. Inspiration is different from motivation (in my mind). Motivation comes from external forces. You've got to make payroll, so you're motivated to close a sale. Or you get to go to Hawaii, so you are motivated to make that happen. Motivation is created by external forces that may be positive or negative. A reward or a penalty.

But inspiration (in my mind), is something that is kindled on the inside. Inspiration happens when you actually see a compelling vision for the future that creates desire to reach that dream. Your dreams fuel your life. No dream, no fuel. No fuel, the vehicle doesn't move.

I am convinced that one of the biggest limiting factors is lack of vision. The lack of a dream equals the lack of desire. When your imagination captures a compelling vision for your life and you connect the success of your business vehicle to it, you now have something to work with.

If there is no dream, why would you want to do the hard work in this book? You wouldn't. And you won't. So you must develop a compelling, inspirational vision for your life. This will create the desire (the fuel) to move your vehicle forward.

Business owners suffer from many distractions, a lack of focus, and a lack of discipline. Many aren't organized or motivated. If that's you, it's because you aren't inspired. If someone called you offering an all-expense-paid trip to Hawaii for two, but you had to leave tomorrow, you would get pretty dog-gone focused and disciplined all of a sudden. You see, that picture of Hawaii created desire. So keep searching for your dream. What would you dream about if you could not fail? What would your perfect day look like?

Finally, stay positive by putting inspirational information into your mind *every day*. Avoid talk radio, television, or conversations that don't inspire you. Don't ignore your family, just try to avoid getting into negative or useless conversation.

When your feet hit the floor each morning, focus on the possibilities rather than the problems. Focus on your goals. Focus on your vision. Every day. Refuse to be negative.

Key #2: Organization

Many years ago, I began a daily habit that serves me well to this day. I started carving out an hour in the mornings to work on my projects—to implement. I call this time my "Time Capsule." This is a capsule of time that I take every day (except Sunday) to focus on my top projects and take action. During this time, I don't take phone calls and I don't get involved in anything but working on my projects. The only person who can contact me during this time is my wife. If you have a key staff member who needs to be able to contact you because you are still working "in" the business, let that person know how to contact you, but to only contact you during that time if it is truly an emergency.

The best time for your Time Capsule is early in the morning before anyone else is awake. Especially if you have young children. Once you get involved in the duties of the day, it's difficult to get back to your quiet time. Make a pact with yourself and impose a rule that you can't do anything else until you've done your Time Capsule. You may groan at having to get up an hour earlier, but I would ask you if your dream is compelling enough. Do you have a dream? What do you get if you take massive action? What will the outcome be if you actually implement the things you need to implement? What is the cost of *not* doing it?

Impose a sense of urgency upon yourself (like the trip to Hawaii) and pretend you are going on vacation tomorrow. Do that every day. Speaking of vacation, I love the beach and one of the things that helps me is to have a trip to the beach planned each quarter. I know that if I work really hard for three months, I have a nice reward at the end of it. Put your vacation in your plan and use that as a source of inspiration.

Focus on the biggest return-on-investment (ROI) projects. Once you've taken the *Born To Win* Business Assessment to see where you are now, pick four projects to build your systems. Pick the four strategies that you know will move your business forward in the next 90 days. Pick those that you know will help you reach your sales goals.

When you get overwhelmed, busy, and distracted, refocus by going back to the Phenomenal Four Projects. Work on those every day during your Time Capsule. Take action on your projects every day.

Key #3: Training

Zig Ziglar said, "You were born to win, but to be the winner you were born to be, you must plan to win and prepare to win before you can expect to win. But if you plan to win and prepare to win, you can expect to win." Training is preparing. Training is learning and practicing these strategies until they are second nature. Continue to practice until you develop the *skill*.

Learning these strategies is a good start, but you've got to get in the ring and spar. You've got to train as hard as you fight. So often small business owners use the strategies incorrectly or they cut corners. You must discipline yourself to learn and flesh out the systems in the real world.

The most important key to implementation. I've saved the best for last. Above all, the last key is the most important. Only the rarest of business owners are successful without this one...

Key #4: Support

Every business owner needs support, encouragement, and accountability.

Support means that you have a group of people around you to help you fulfill your vision, mission, and purpose. This will include your staff, but also should include your peers, and you need a coach.

Encouragement means that you have a group of people around you who remind you that you can do it. Zig Ziglar said, "Encouragement is the fuel people run on." I am so grateful for those around me who show me that I can do more than I can ask, think, or imagine.

Accountability means that you have a group of people who are there to ask you the tough questions. Have you done what you need to do this week to reach your goals? Are you staying focused on your goals? Are you working your plan? Are you developing your systems? Accountability is huge. I am so grateful for those people who are tough enough to ask the tough questions. I don't always like it, but no pain, no gain.

I am so grateful for the mentors, coaches, and consultants I have been blessed with in my life and business. We need people who have our best interest at heart, not just someone who has knowledge. You can be inspired, organized, and have the best strategies, and still not implement. The reason? You work for yourself. You aren't accountable to anyone. You may not be getting the support and encouragement you need from those closest to you.

If you're like me, I've worn my wife's ears off with business stuff for over 28 years. One day I had a big dream that came to my mind. It was a doozy! I was standing in the kitchen unloading the dishwasher (I unload, she loads—that's our deal). As this dream came to me, I began to share it with my wife. It was so big and so exciting that as I shared it with my wife, I had my eyes closed and both my hands in the air. I said, "Honey, I see us doing..." as I drew the picture of the dream in my mind. She had her hands on her hips, tapping her foot, and when I finished she said, "I've got a dream too, of you unloading that dishwasher right there!"

Don't get me wrong, my wife has been my biggest supporter. It was a friend of her family from whom I got my original idea. She gave me my first Rolodex (remember those?). She referred her friends to me. She was very successful in sales and helped me make payroll many times. She went out and worked with me. She endured my foolish escapades and massive debt build up. But as she says, "I always knew you had potential, it just took a long time to train you!"

In many cases, the business owner has drawn the spouse into the business, and the working relationship isn't very positive. The challenges of the business are brought home to the dinner table. This creates many pressures.

Other business owners are helpful, but don't have the skill to lead us where we need to go. They can share helpful strategies and resources, but they don't get paid to keep us accountable.

You need a coach. Professional athletes have a coach. In fact, they have more than one. They have coaches for specific areas.

As mentioned previously, the original definition of a coach came from a carriage—a medium to get you from where you are to where you want to go. Think of the stage coach of the Old West. Small business owners desperately need coaches in their lives to support them, to encourage them, and to hold them accountable.

I've used many coaches and consultants in my career. I shudder to think where I would be without the support, encouragement, and accountability of my coaches. When my company was in a financial mess, I reached out to my good friend Ellen Rohr. As a consultant, she came in and helped us get our financial system in order. This is what I needed. Hands-on help to keep me accountable to the goal that I said I wanted.

Another example is Mark Ehrlich. Several years ago I felt I needed someone I could rely on to help me get where I wanted to go. Someone who had already been there or had walked with someone who had. Mark had worked on and off with Michael Gerber since 1977. I first met Mark when Michael spoke at my conference the first time. Mark helped me find my unique gifts and held me accountable to the dream I had. Both these people made a tremendous difference in my life and business.

About nine years ago I got really healthy. I lost 50 pounds and became very fit. I had a certified nutritionist who taught me what to eat and when. As long as I did what she said to do, it worked. I saw her on a regular basis and that kept me accountable to eating right. I had a personal trainer who came three days a week. I was so fit that I could easily do 50 push-ups. I was lean and very strong.

But then I did something really dumb. I got bored with my trainer, and I didn't want to work for it anymore. My trainer was frustrated because I wouldn't do the work. I got lazy. Before too long, I stopped training. I figured I would do it myself. I play extreme basketball every Sunday, and I figured I could find a place to play basketball (something I loved rather than the boring routine of strength training) a few times a week. I could ride my bike.

How do you think that went? Not good. It wasn't long before my legs got weak, and I blew out my knee playing basketball and had to have surgery. This put me out for over six months. I started gaining weight, feeling lethargic again, and began cheating on my diet (I was now having my supplements shipped rather than meeting regularly with my nutritionist). The end result, my gut began to grow back.

At this writing, my weight is still down by 25 pounds, and I'm relatively healthy. I still eat pretty healthy foods, and I exercise by playing basketball, walking, and riding my bike. But it's not the same. I want to be super fit, not just average.

What about you?

Do you want to be *phenomenally* successful in your business? Or just marginal. Have you tried to go it alone for too long? Have you proven that you need support, encouragement, and accountability? Have you proven that you most likely won't do the things you need to do? Are you ready for support, encouragement, and accountability?

If your answer is "yes," I have some phenomenal news for you…*Phenomenal PODS.*™

The driving force behind the massive success small business owners are having around the world with my systems is due to a process I call PODS™ (Power Of Discovery Systems™). Our members meet in small groups of less than 12 people every week over the phone to get support, encouragement, and accountability. Each member reports what they have implemented for the week. The coach gives feedback (support), gives them a pat on the back (encouragement), and asks them about the goals they said they wanted to achieve (accountability).

I have found this to be an *extremely effective* method for long-term implementation. During this process a number of amazing things take place:

1. *Members are accountable.* They commit to implement the things they said they wanted to accomplish. After all, who wants to show up and admit to the group that they didn't do anything? No one.

2. *Members get feedback.* When members implement, they get validation, feedback, and "Way to go!" Who wants that? Everyone! As Zig said, this is the fuel we run on. We don't get enough encouragement as small business owners. We just get to deal with all the problems.

3. *Members discover they aren't alone.* Other business owners are dealing with the same challenges they are.

4. *Members are encouraged* by success stories—when someone on the call has a breakthrough, it is shared with the other members on the call.

5. *The Power Of Discovery.* The biggest advantage of small groups is that the facilitator doesn't teach. Instead he or she *facilitates.* As the group processes the open-ended questions and report in, they "discover" things. And when you find something, you own it.

The power is in the fact that no one told you that you had to do something. You discovered it on your own. When you discover it, you are much more likely to implement. The facilitator and the group are there to spur you on—to support you, to encourage you, and to hold you accountable to the things to which you want to be held accountable.

6. *Community is created.* The most wonderful thing about PODS™ is that the group develops a sense of community—that we are on this journey together. This sense of belonging is deepened as our members attend our live conferences. They build friendships, compare notes on how they are implementing the systems, and they care for one another.

7. *Massive business growth and life change.* The PODS™ coupled with learning these systems is revolutionizing small businesses around the world. The success stories are truly *phenomenal!*

See Phenomenal Testimonials of PODS Members at
www.HowardPartridgeInnerCircle.com

Acknowledgments

Thank you to Almighty God for allowing me to do what I do and giving me the Grace to do it.

Thank you to Denise and Christian for your love and support through all of my projects.

Thank you to my phenomenal staff who LIVE this book every day. It would not be possible without you.

Thank you to my friend and brother Tom Ziglar for helping me think through and flesh out these business concepts - and extending my platform, proving they work in any business.

Thank you to our phenomenal coaches for your leadership.

Thank you to all of our coaching members. We learn just as much from you as you do from us. Your love for me and one another is astounding.

About the Author

Howard Partridge grew up on welfare in Mobile Alabama and left home at 18. He arrived in Houston, Texas on a Greyhound bus with only 25 cents in his pocket.

At age 23, he started his first business out of the trunk of his car and built it up to a multi-million dollar enterprise. He has owned 9 small businesses altogether and owns 4 companies at the time of this printing.

He is president of Phenomenal Products, Inc. which helps small business owners stop being slaves to their business by transforming it into a predictable, profitable, turnkey operation.

For the past 16 years Howard has helped small business owners around the world dramatically improve their businesses. He currently has coaching members worldwide, is the exclusive small business coach for the Zig Ziglar corporation, and is a founding member of the John Maxwell Coaching Team.

Howard has led hundreds of seminars, webinars, workshops and holds his own live multi-day events which have featured some of America's top business trainers including Michael Gerber, Bob Burg, Dr. Joseph A. Michelli, and American legend Zig Ziglar.

Howard is married to Denise and has one beautiful son, Christian who is a freshman at Texas Tech University in Lubbock, Texas.